Grown-Up
Leadership
workbook

Grown-Up Leadership
workbook

Leigh Bailey

All other inquiries should be addressed to:

Leigh Bailey
lbailey@thebaileygroup.com
Martha Carlson
mcarlson@thebaileygroup.com

Printed in USA

ISBN 90-77256-15-6

Contents

ACKNOWLEDGMENTS

It is truly exciting to introduce the new *Grown-Up Leadership Workbook*. This workbook is the result of collaboration with many colleagues, and I want to take a minute to acknowledge them and their contributions.

First, I want to acknowledge the contributions of Maureen Bailey, co-author of the original *Grown-Up Leadership* book, upon which this new workbook is based. Her voice in *Grown-Up Leadership* is an inextricable part of this new work.

Thank you to the many leaders that I have been privileged to work with as an executive coach and a consultant in leadership. I hope that this workbook is a faithful reflection of all that they have taught me over the past seventeen years.

I also want to thank Astrid De Deyne, Kathe Grooms, Molly Grooms, John Kelley, and Karien Sticker at Nova Vista Publishing for being partners in this effort and for their invaluable contributions to the manuscript and to the design of the workbook.

Finally, I want to particularly acknowledge Martha Carlson's contributions to the *Grown-Up Leadership Workbook*. She has shepherded it from its early rough stages to its final form and made countless original, creative contributions to the workbook. Thanks, Martha, for your invaluable contribution.

LEIGH H. BAILEY, M.A.
The Bailey Consulting Group

TEACHING AND LEARNING ABOUT LEADERSHIP

"No leader is ever fully realized. At most, one can observe individuals who are in the course of attaining greater skills and heightened effectiveness."
HOWARD GARDNER

Many leaders are praised for being bottom-line driven – working to achieve success at any cost. But they also leave behind a trail of unhappy employees, motivated by fear and more focused on finding their next job than on improving their performance. Leaders who fail to bring maturity to their day-to-day work cannot succeed in the long run, because they continually alienate people. They are dinosaurs in today's business world.

In our work as leadership coaches, we have observed many qualities and skills that contribute to effective leadership. Foremost among them is a level of self-awareness and maturity that comes as a result of commitment to personal development. Not every leader buys into the link between enlightenment and business. But we have seen hundreds of cases where failing to grow up keeps leaders stuck in habitual, reactive behavior based on childhood or family-based demons and prevents them from achieving their business objectives.

In our view, the 21st century's business world challenges leaders to be masters in the art of human development. As a leader, you must assess your own abilities and seek out tools that specifically enhance your personal development. That's where we come in, as leadership coaches. By supporting the *personal* growth of our clients, we help them address their leadership challenges. We see, in the results of our holistic approach to leadership, changes in our clients' lives that give them their best chances of success today. We therefore encourage you to actively use this workbook to help you examine yourself, and to develop yourself further in ways that support your success as a leader.

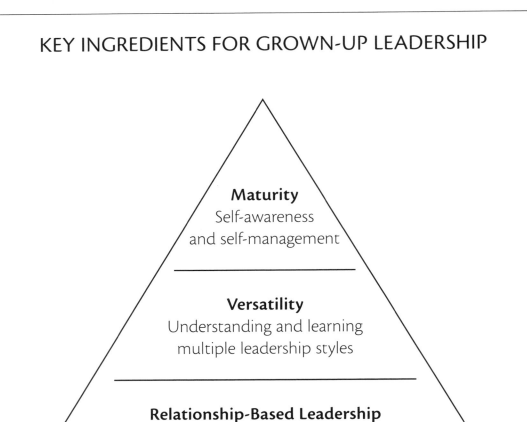

KEY INGREDIENTS FOR GROWN-UP LEADERSHIP

Maturity
Self-awareness
and self-management

Versatility
Understanding and learning
multiple leadership styles

Relationship-Based Leadership
Engaging others

We believe that the key ingredients for exceptional leadership include:

- **Maturity:** the courage to develop self-awareness and understanding, and to make changes when you discover personal barriers
- **Versatility:** the ability to understand and learn other leadership styles
- **Relationship-based leadership:** the willingness to engage others to get results

When leaders have these assets, they become great coaches and team-builders.

In the coming pages, we will examine leadership in many ways, but most importantly as it influences the behavior of others. Being grown up takes you a long way toward leading effectively. That may seem obvious, yet it continually amazes us to hear how many leaders act childishly. Putting it bluntly, people deserve grown-up leaders! We aim to give you the skills and abilities we've seen in the best leaders among us, to help you join that group.

SITTING AT THE GROWN-UP TABLE

We talk about *Grown-Up Leadership* partly because for us, it conjures up images of giant family dinners. Adults typically sit at the grown-up table in the dining room, while young children are relegated to a table in the kitchen or family room. To be invited to sit with the grownups is an honor, but it also requires good manners. Childish behavior is not tolerated at the grown-up table.

This metaphor works because, in fact, some leaders among us still act like they're sitting at the kids' table. They lose control of their emotions, keep their "me-first" mentality, bully others, or act dishonestly. If we don't tolerate such behavior at the grown-up table at home, why should we tolerate it among our leaders?

Think about how hard it is to be around adults who still act in childish ways. Then imagine how hard it is to have a boss who behaves immaturely. It's a nightmare: you feel frustrated, demotivated, and may look for another job. In contrast, working for a grown-up boss can be a dream: you give your very best and feel fulfilled and appreciated. But make no mistake – leaders who are grownups have worked hard to mature into healthy individuals. They have learned how to manage relationships with others, can make workplaces feel positive, and motivate employees to increase productivity.

WHAT DOES – AND DOESN'T – WORK

Based on our experience, organizations that encourage their leaders to become grownups see bottom-line results. Leaders who have a healthy sense of self-worth, a strong curiosity about people and things, and an acute awareness of both their own and others' feelings – all qualities of maturity – succeed by actively engaging employees, establishing creative and productive work environments, and achieving board room objectives as well.

But you may be wondering: What about organizations that have not come to recognize the importance of grown-up leadership? In our experience, they continue to hire people at key leadership levels who are stuck in immature behavior patterns that sabotage their missions and make people leave. Believe us – we have worked with many leaders who:

- Procrastinate
- Feel crushed by their workload
- Appear unable to connect with their co-workers
- Struggle to contain their anger or frustration at co-workers
- Act like they know it all, but confide to us that they secretly believe they are imposters
- Are jealous of the successes of their co-workers and employees
- Are unable to sustain meaningful, trusting relationships with colleagues

Employees should not have to deal with such immature behavior.

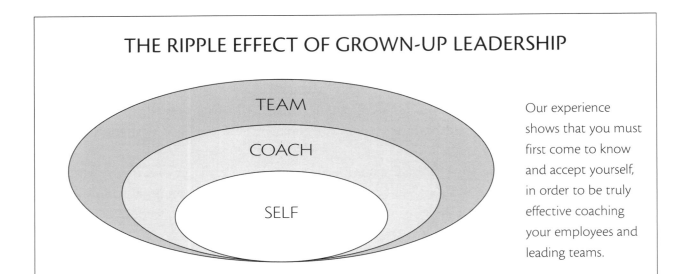

THE RIPPLE EFFECT OF GROWN-UP LEADERSHIP

TEAM

COACH

SELF

Our experience shows that you must first come to know and accept yourself, in order to be truly effective coaching your employees and leading teams.

Leadership requires outgrowing such immaturity, and gaining the skills required to sit at the grown-up table. Getting in touch with yourself, and learning to observe your own actions and behavior with curiosity and objectivity, will help you gain the capacity you need to make the kind of changes that great leaders make. Such self-awareness can be painful at first, but will translate into results that you, your employees, your peers, and your superiors will definitely notice.

In the course of this workbook we will take you through a progression of discussions and exercises that will help you to develop yourself, but then also help you direct your leadership skills to people you lead, coaching them to be their best. We will give you insights and tips that will help you get the best out of teams as well. The ripple effect, radiating out from your work on yourself, will be evident throughout our discussions.

On the next page you will find an exercise to help you think about what makes a leader effective. Take a few minutes to think about your situation today before filling it out.

OBJECTIVES

By completing *The Grown-Up Leadership Workbook* you will:

- Demonstrate greater maturity and versatility in your approach to leadership
- Act intentionally and purposefully to create a climate that promotes employee engagement, achievement and creative excellence
- Think and act purposefully to achieve results and create and sustain effective individual and team relationships

Personal Reflections on Leadership

Answer the questions below, using any format that is comfortable, e.g., bullet-points, statements, paragraphs, individual words, etc.

1. Think about the most effective leader you've had in your career or from other experiences in your past. What characteristics made him or her effective?

2. Think about the most ineffective leader you've had. What characteristics made him or her ineffective?

3. Are great leaders born or made?

4. What is the biggest leadership challenge you are currently facing?

5. What do you expect to gain from your investment in your leadership development?

WORKBOOK ORGANIZATION

The *Grown Up Leadership Workbook* is organized in sections:

Section 1:   Maturity   Gaining maturity as a leader through
                                                awareness, acceptance, and action

Section 2:   Versatility   Becoming more adept at using a variety of
                                                interaction styles and skills to lead more
                                                effectively

Section 3:   Relationship-Based   Enhancing your ability to engage and develop
              Leadership: Coaching   employees through one-on-one relationships
                                                and effective coaching

Section 4:   Relationship-Based   Building and leading high performing teams
              Leadership: Team Effectiveness

Section 5:   A Model for Personal Change   Taking action to increase maturity, versatility,
                                                and relationship-based leadership skills

Section 6:   The Role of a Leader   Practicing grown-up leadership and becoming
                                                a grown-up leader

Section 7:   Resources   Additional assessments, information,
                                                a bibliography and other resources

Each section includes Personal Coaching Sessions designed to engage you in the process of
becoming a grown-up leader.

SECTION 1
MATURITY

"It takes more courage to reveal insecurities than to hide them, more strength to relate to people than to dominate them... to abide by thought-out principles rather than blind reflex."

A. KARRAS

TURN AND LOOK

Being grown up is important for all adults, but it's a vital trait in an outstanding leader. While people grow and mature differently, those who strive to become great leaders need to recognize situations in life that offer opportunities for learning about themselves. Leaders whose actions are controlled by personal fears and anxieties can seem petty, judgmental, inconsistent, and even immature to their co-workers. Such behavior is the result of old, comfortable, yet destructive habits. To overcome these habits, you must try new behaviors, which can cause you to feel unsure, insecure and vulnerable – at least at the start.

Don't be fooled: being grown up does not require perfection. In fact, as you gain maturity, you will recognize and accept your own imperfections and the limitations of others. This process – becoming more aware of our imperfections – is often humbling. But as you will see, such self-examination is extremely valuable to you as a leader.

Exploring your past objectively and remaining committed to the process can bring to the surface painful emotions, such as fear, sadness, anger, or loneliness, that you thought you'd left behind. Accepting the challenge of experiencing these emotions is a giant step towards greater maturity and leadership effectiveness, but a difficult one nonetheless.

RECOGNIZING THE POWER OF PERCEPTION

Few things are true of all of us, except this: we all are human. As humans, we carry a lifetime of experiences in our memories, dating back to early childhood. Experiences influence our beliefs, the way we respond to outside stimuli, and certainly, the way we relate to others. The person each of us is today is the sum of our genetic inheritance and life history. And it's impossible to separate our private selves from our working selves.

So, much as it pains most of us to admit it, life experience – and family experience – impact the ways we act as leaders in the workplace. Most work situations are hierarchical systems. As such, they are fertile grounds that reactivate our old beliefs, values, issues with authority, and concerns regarding self-esteem and self-worth.

Let's consider, for example, the approval-seeking nature of most work environments. Early in our careers, we must seek approval from others (particularly superiors) in order to make a place for ourselves and to be noticed for future promotions. This normal approval-seeking process echoes experiences with parents and other authority figures from the past, and unresolved resentments and fears from childhood can resurface as a result.

If this sounds like a psychology primer, then you are starting to grasp the link we make

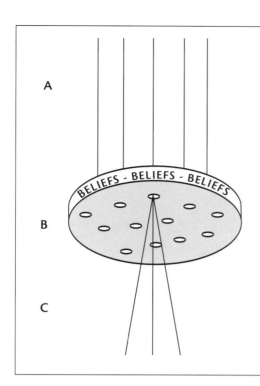

ALBERT ELLIS' STRUCTURE OF INTERPRETATION (ABC MODEL)

Activating Events (A)

Outside events that we respond to daily.

Beliefs (B)

The belief systems through which we filter those events – our own emotions and thoughts that happen inside of us as we process these experiences. These beliefs can be either rational or irrational.

Consequences (C)

The internal and external consequences of A and B: how we think, feel and behave in response to those activating events.

between your personal development experiences (your psychological development) and your growth as a leader.

In this area, we appreciate the work of Albert Ellis, a prominent expert in cognitive-behavioral psychology, who pioneered in understanding the connection between past experience and present behavior. Ellis studied the process of connecting inside beliefs with outside events in an effort to gain insight into why people think, feel, and behave as they do in certain situations. According to Ellis, the process starts with **A**, an *activating event*, or an everyday occurrence that we respond to – like an encounter with a co-worker, a traffic incident, or an unexpected phone call.

We filter these events, Ellis suggests, through **B**, a set of *beliefs* that affect how we see the world: our own unique collection of history and experiences. Think of this belief system as a prism through which we view the world. It is this prism, rather than the activating events themselves, that is most responsible for **C**, the *consequences* of a given activating event. According to Ellis, the way we act – in life, in relationships, and in work situations – is based on this ABC Model.

Here's the rub. Many beliefs, especially those developed as ways of coping with perceived threats to our personal safety and self-esteem in the past, have outlived their usefulness. And if we study a group of leaders, we see that there are considerable differences between the beliefs of the effective and ineffective leaders among them.

We regularly meet people in leadership positions who continue to apply childhood rules (or habits) that have long since outlived their usefulness. These habitual, protective responses can be hurtful, destructive and ineffective, and tend to override healthy leadership responses. When we react out of habit, we reduce the likelihood that we'll accomplish our present-day objectives.

BECOMING CONSCIOUS OF YOUR UNCONSCIOUS

The difficult journey through the land of self-examination takes great courage. Many people feel quite uncomfortable when they start to learn about themselves, either through self-examination or through some unexpected feedback from a co-worker or friend. They feel exposed, child-like, and often, ashamed. Letting go of habitual, protective behaviors is like going into a battle without armor, and that's a scary notion.

But this process offers many rewards as well. In the 1960s, Abraham Maslow popularized the concept of *self-actualization*, which he defined as having a healthy sense of self-worth and self-trust, a strong curiosity about people, and an acute awareness of both one's own and others' thoughts and feelings. We call this process "growing up." The process of maturing as a human being requires an inside-out examination of one's belief system, revisiting old memories, pondering past experiences, examining relationships, and gaining insight into the filter or prism through which one views outside experiences. Those who can navigate this process will gain new tools that will help them lead others effectively.

There are many ways you can gain insight into how you perceive your world. Recognizing the prism through which you look is an important starting point for transforming your personal awareness and effectiveness. We will discuss other approaches in upcoming sections.

In the exercise that follows, you will begin gathering data about early influences and experiences that can be processed as we continue through this workbook together. To do it, you will need a quiet, comfortable place to write, a notebook, and your favorite pen.

Personal Prism Exercise

STEP ONE: PERSONAL HISTORY

Take a few minutes to write answers to the questions below about your personal history. Focus on these questions one by one, pause, and then write a few words to capture your thoughts. Your personal prism of beliefs and experiences colors your responses to events, every single day. If you become self-aware and recognize your prism at work, your growth as a leader will come faster. This exercise will be a cornerstone for a lot of your work in later sections of this workbook, so take as much time and care with it as you possibly can.

BIRTH

* Where were you born?

* How would you describe the culture and values of the community (i.e., city, small town, farm) where you grew up?

* How would you describe the family you were born into?

WORK

* Which members of your family worked during your childhood? How much?

* Did they like their work? Did they have a sense of purpose? Were they successful?

* What early messages did you receive from your family about work?

SIBLINGS

* Are you an only child or do you have siblings? If you have siblings, where are you in the birth order of your family?

* What roles did you play in your relationships with your siblings, if any (e.g., leader, peacemaker)? If you are an only child, how did that shape your behavior?

* In what ways do you play the same role(s) as an adult?

AUTHORITY

* Who was in charge in your family? How would you describe his or her leadership style?

* What other authority figures played significant roles in your childhood? What impacts did they have?

VALUES AND RELIGION

* Who were some individuals or institutions that your family members liked, respected or admired?

* What types of people did your family members criticize?

* Were family members optimistic or pessimistic? How did that affect your beliefs or behavior?

* What beliefs about religion affect your behavior?

* What role did religion play in your upbringing?

FINANCIAL

* What role did money play in your family?

* How were financial issues discussed?

* Who had input into financial decisions?

TEMPERAMENT AND EMOTIONS

* What emotions were visible or tolerated in your family? What emotions were not visible or tolerated? By whom?

* When thinking about your childhood, what emotions do you recall most strongly?

* How did others describe you as a child?

CONFLICT

* What happened when people disagreed in your family?

* Was conflict encouraged, discouraged or tolerated?

NURTURING

* What was the safest way for you to express a need, desire, idea, or goal as a child?

* Who was the most likely to support what you asked for?

* How did you get your emotional needs met?

STEP TWO: REFLECTION

Review your answers and try to identify the insights you gained. Are there any people you'd like to talk with to further explore your personal prism? Save your insights for your future work.

MEET THE ACCOMMODATOR AND THE INTIMIDATOR

Our process also recognizes that there are different *types* of people, whose styles look dramatically different in leadership positions. Most individuals lean in one of two directions. One is an Accomodator: a compliant person who is comfortable with an empowering approach. The other is an Intimidator: a more aggressive person who tends to use a forceful approach. Both of these styles or tendencies result from your upbringing, experiences and preferences.

UNDERSTANDING YOUR MOTIVATIONS – ARE YOU AN ACCOMMODATOR OR AN INTIMIDATOR?

Why is it important to know if you are an Accommodator or Intimidator? Because most people fall into styles of habitual behavior without even thinking about it. And that's when we are least effective at accomplishing our objectives, because these habits get in the way of success.

Many leaders have a vague awareness of their struggles, but find it hard to articulate them. Those who learn to describe their challenges also understand them more clearly. They know more about the sources of their behavior, and are in a better position to begin making changes.

CHARACTERISTICS OF ACCOMMODATORS AND INTIMIDATORS

If you look around you, and also at yourself, you'll quickly perceive the two clusters of tendencies that Accommodators and Intimidators tend to exhibit.

The Accommodator
- Shows an excessive need to be liked, wanted, loved, welcomed
- Values safety in the extreme
- Is highly affected by expectations and opinions of others
- Prefers to stay out of the limelight
- Tends to be policy- and procedure-driven: follows the rules first
- Secret motto: "I don't trust myself, so I will follow you."

The Intimidator
- Mistrusts others
- Assumes that the world is a jungle and that life is a contest of "survival of the fittest"
- Believes the best defense is a good offense
- Knows how to fight
- Is sometimes emotionally inhibited, uncomfortable talking about feelings
- Shows a strong need to be recognized, affirmed and praised
- Secret motto: "I don't trust you, so I will fight you to get what I need."

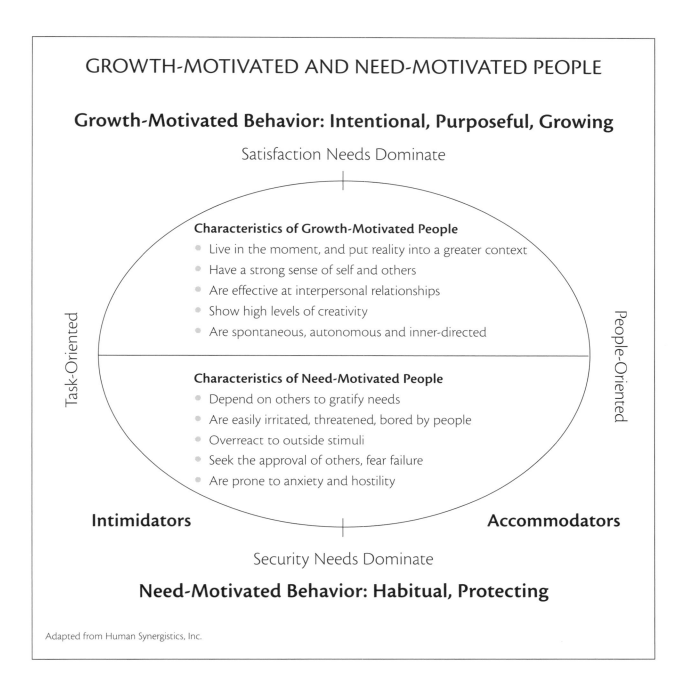

GROWTH-MOTIVATED AND NEED-MOTIVATED PEOPLE

Growth-Motivated Behavior: Intentional, Purposeful, Growing

Satisfaction Needs Dominate

Characteristics of Growth-Motivated People
- Live in the moment, and put reality into a greater context
- Have a strong sense of self and others
- Are effective at interpersonal relationships
- Show high levels of creativity
- Are spontaneous, autonomous and inner-directed

Characteristics of Need-Motivated People
- Depend on others to gratify needs
- Are easily irritated, threatened, bored by people
- Overreact to outside stimuli
- Seek the approval of others, fear failure
- Are prone to anxiety and hostility

Task-Oriented

People-Oriented

Intimidators

Accommodators

Security Needs Dominate

Need-Motivated Behavior: Habitual, Protecting

Adapted from Human Synergistics, Inc.

The graphic above shows how Accomodators, who tend to move away from others, and Intimidators, who tend to move against others, are both need-motivated, with an emphasis on security. They tend to depend too much on the outside environment to meet their needs rather than meeting needs through a healthy sense of themselves.

As people (and leaders) mature, they are more motivated by growth and the drive for satisfaction dominates. As you consider the characteristics of Accommodators and Intimidators, think about their capacity as leaders. How does increasing maturity impact this capacity?

In the exercise on the following pages, you will have an opportunity to assess your own leadership style and tendency.

Assessing Your Leadership Style

Here's an exercise to assess your own leadership tendencies. Review the list of ways people cope when under particular stress below. Circle the characteristics that fit you. At the end, you should be able to tell if you tend to be an Accommodator or an Intimidator.

STEP ONE

Please look at this list of statements and circle all that apply to you:

1. Hesitant to express opinion or be in the spotlight
2. Critical, mistrustful of others – consider others incompetent
3. Want to be liked by others
4. Prefer to stand out in a crowd
5. Often willing to put needs of others before your own needs
6. Like having the attention of others
7. Wait for others to make difficult decisions rather than being proactive
8. Prefer to be the one in charge
9. Know and follow rules carefully
10. Question the input or suggestions of others
11. Avoid confrontation
12. Able to say "no" to requests and ideas
13. Have doubts about your own level of competency
14. Cause confrontation
15. Tend to assume that others are more competent
16. Prefer to be alone in the limelight
17. Easier to say "yes" than "no" to others
18. Winning is a priority, despite any costs
19. Want to be included in others' projects or conversations
20. Likely to focus on minute details of a project or situation
21. Feel hyper-anxiety in situations most others experience as non-threatening
22. Try to be unrealistically precise

STEP TWO

Now, tally the number of odd-numbered responses that you circled, and compare that to the number of even-numbered responses you chose. If you have more odd-numbered items, then you probably tend to be an Accommodator, while if you have more even-numbered items, you probably tend to be an Intimidator.

STEP THREE

Take a walk, sit with a cup of tea, or make time to consider this new information.

- What is your tendency: Accommodator or Intimidator?

- How does this information fit with what you know about yourself?

- What feedback, events, conversations, or personal concerns of the last year fit with or don't match this tendency?

Knowing your own tendency will be very helpful in our future discussions.

GOING ONE STEP FURTHER

Completing the exercise above will help you begin the important process of understanding yourself, your behaviors and your leadership tendencies. When we work with our clients, we often use assessment tools that help them gain an even greater perspective on their thinking and preferences. If you choose to do more in-depth work, we recommend two assessment tools:

Myers Briggs Type Indicator (MBTI)

Carl Jung's theory of psychological type was made available by Isabel Myers and Katharine Briggs through the MBTI. It is a research-tested tool and model for helping leaders understand both themselves and others. The MBTI provides a non-judgmental lens through which a leader gains a deeper understanding of how people differ in the way they take in information, communicate, and make decisions. Insight into those differences helps a leader to value diversity in a variety of forms. It also provides tools and a greater sophistication for working with others.

The Life Styles Inventory (LSI)

This thinking styles assessment, developed by Clayton Lafferty, helps leaders identify their existing thinking styles and suggests specific ways to enhance their leadership effectiveness. Specifically, Lafferty's research has found that thinking styles that emphasize achievement, self-acceptance and developing supportive relationships lead to long-term success as a leader. The LSI includes both modules for self-assessment and for getting feedback from other individuals.

THE SKILL OF SELF-OBSERVATION

As a step in transforming awareness into enhanced leadership effectiveness, we must become tolerant, or even accepting, of the parts of ourselves that we dislike. Why is this so important?

Leaders believe in their own opinions more than in the opinions of others. But the process of change takes more than merely intellectual awareness. For real change to occur, you must *accept* what you have become aware of and make the awareness yours, at both a gut level and an intellectual level.

How do you move beyond mere intellectual awareness? The process requires de-sensitizing yourself to the emotional experience of observing your particular *need-based style* in your day-to-day behavior. The ability to take a step back, and to observe your thoughts and actions from a detached perspective, is a skill we call "self-observation."

IMPROVING YOUR SELF-OBSERVATION

You will learn a great deal and gain maturity if you can improve your self-observation regarding your leadership style. Here are some important insights that can help you embrace this learning process. Think of them as self-talk, or affirmations, that you can use for support and encouragement as you proceed:

- I can observe my emotional reactions without acting on them or being held hostage by them.
- I can rationally look at situations without being overwhelmed by my emotions.
- I can learn to tolerate emotional discomfort without pushing it away.
- I can choose how I respond to activating events, rather than reacting to them out of old habit.

As we have discussed, the journey through awareness and acceptance requires you to recognize the sources of your inner beliefs and demons. You also must make conscious choices about behaviors that are constructive and ones that are destructive. The journey includes the process of recognizing the work we do to appease others (as Accommodators) or control them (as Intimidators). With that insight, you can move bit by bit away from need-based motivation to the motivation that comes from your true self.

A MODEL FOR CHANGE

Real, lasting change is gradual, a process rather than an event. The change process requires learning about your beliefs and taking steps to overcome those that have become barriers in your life. We use a personal change model with our clients called Awareness-Acceptance-Action. The most successful of our clients – particularly those who make changes in their lives and then sustain them – follow this model for change.

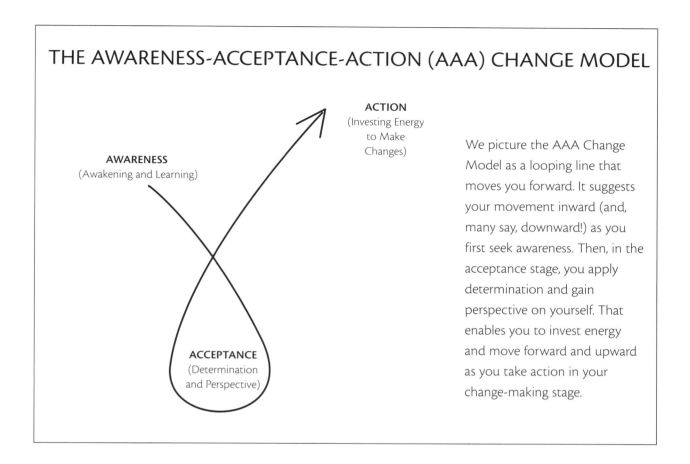

THE AWARENESS-ACCEPTANCE-ACTION (AAA) CHANGE MODEL

ACTION
(Investing Energy to Make Changes)

AWARENESS
(Awakening and Learning)

ACCEPTANCE
(Determination and Perspective)

We picture the AAA Change Model as a looping line that moves you forward. It suggests your movement inward (and, many say, downward!) as you first seek awareness. Then, in the acceptance stage, you apply determination and gain perspective on yourself. That enables you to invest energy and move forward and upward as you take action in your change-making stage.

AWARENESS: AWAKENING AND LEARNING

Many who choose to lead are high achievers – individuals who push themselves to accomplish, who strive for personal excellence. Some even become compulsive in their pursuit of achievement. But when high achievers are confronted with their deficiencies, and begin to learn how those deficiencies contribute to their shortcomings as leaders, their motivation to achieve often turns into unnecessarily harsh self-criticism. Through *Awareness* we learn about our own behaviors, awakening to aspects of ourselves that were previously hidden from us. As our eyes open, we begin to gain more perspective on our own behavior.

ACCEPTANCE: DETERMINATION AND PERSPECTIVE

Acceptance, the second stage of our change model, helps us become gentler with ourselves by teaching us to detach, step back, and look at our issues more objectively. We begin to move beyond embarrassment and guilt, and to gradually realize that there are more productive alternatives to our troublesome behaviors. By becoming more skillful at self-observation and recognizing choices we can make, we see how outmoded behavior keeps us from being our best selves. More importantly, we start to learn how we can change.

Acceptance means becoming less embarrassed about old behaviors, and instead, growing curious about them. Success in this stage requires that you develop personal persistence to learn more about yourself, your beliefs and your actions. When you find a loose thread of information, you can push yourself to learn how that thread has run through your life. During the acceptance stage, you might also risk becoming more personally revealing, confiding and then exploring your discoveries with others. The rewards can be amazingly rich.

ACTION: INVESTING ENERGY TO MAKE CHANGES

At work, acceptance often makes us realize that sometimes, old behaviors keep us from achieving our objectives. It's time to commit to investigating them, then to learn other ways of behaving and break those old, ineffective habits. As we start to experiment with new behaviors, we will develop strategies to enhance strengths and to deal with weaknesses. In short, we start to take *Action* to grow up as individuals and as leaders.

Action goes well beyond learning about yourself. At some point, you can learn only so much, ponder new options, examine old behaviors, and think about situations differently. Action requires the energy to do something new, to experiment with new behaviors, and to consider changes from the inside out.

RESULTS FROM YOUR AAA WORK

What results can you expect from investing in this AAA process? When working with our clients, we try to help them measure success in small accomplishments, gradually building up a history of awareness and action using the AAA change model. Over time, leaders report that these small successes start to have big impacts. Read on, work hard, and you'll begin to recognize that these are the moments of transition into grown-up leadership.

As you move through the AAA process, you gain insight into your more extreme tendencies and begin to take actions to moderate them. Hopefully, a new era begins, one in which you become more comfortable in your own skin and feel like you belong at the grown-up table. This middle area represents growth for both Accommodators and Intimidators alike, a place where you can connect better with people, and be more honest, respectful, and authentic.

In the exercise on the following page you will begin developing your own plan to increase your awareness and acceptance of your current leadership tendencies.

Developing Your Plan for Awareness and Acceptance

The goal of this growth exercise is to increase your awareness and acceptance of your current thinking and behavior, and to increase your determination to make changes if you so choose. This is best accomplished as part of a gradual, ongoing process that takes place regularly over the coming weeks. You will find that successfully working through introspective exercises such as this can dramatically help you move towards greater maturity as a leader. Later in this workbook you will have a chance to set goals for taking action based on the outcomes of this excercise.

Your daily awareness and acceptance log

Set aside at least 15 minutes a day for the next two weeks. (Put a daily reminder into your PDA or calendar.) Some prefer to make time just after they wake up or before they go to sleep, while others prefer to block out the beginning or end of their workday. What's important is to make time available daily for personal reflection. We recommend devoting a separate notebook to this project.

Having gone through the self-assessment exercise in Section 1 to determine whether your personal behavior style is skewed either towards the Accommodator or the Intimidator, write the answers to the following four questions into your notebook each day:

* What personal actions or behaviors did you notice in the past day that demonstrate your tendencies toward an accommodating or intimidating style?

* What were you thinking, remembering, or feeling when those situations arose?

- What impact did these thoughts or feelings have on that situation?

- How did your actions in those situations affect the outcome you wanted?

SECTION 2
VERSATILITY

"When all you have is a hammer, everything tends to look like a nail."
ABRAHAM MASLOW

LEADERSHIP VERSATILITY: BUILDING A BIGGER TOOLBOX

Grown-up leaders expand beyond their natural skills in order to achieve exceptional success. Motivating, coaching and developing others requires you to make a clear commitment to learning new skills. As we have discussed, your personal development is a key step. In this chapter we examine another quality of grown-up leadership: versatility.

A WIDER RANGE OF SKILLS

To keep your home in good repair, you need a full tool kit to handle the variety of jobs that you face. Likewise, those who lead others need to have a wide range of appropriate, effective tools in their leadership toolboxes. Because even if you own the best hammer on the market, you won't be able to fix or improve something that requires a monkey wrench.

To be well equipped to lead in a grown-up way, you need to be adept at using a variety of interaction styles and skills. For most people, one style of relating to others comes most naturally, feels the most comfortable, and gives them the greatest confidence. But growing up as a leader requires adding complementary skills. This process of gaining *versatility* can at first feel unnatural and quite difficult. But you will need these new tools if you want to be able to reach a higher level of leadership success.

By now you have developed a better understanding of your own beliefs, your personal prism through which you see the world. Having become more aware of that prism, you have gotten better at recognizing how it affects you in your work and personal life. Hopefully, you have accepted that your own style isn't inherently good or bad, but simply a reality for you.

Just as you have a natural personal style, you have a natural leadership style as well. We notice that most Accommodators tend to prefer an empowering style, while most Intimidators are more comfortable using a forceful leadership approach. Both empowering and forceful leadership styles have numerous positive qualities, but both have potential drawbacks as well.

If you think about leaders you have admired, you'll notice that most mature leaders use both leadership styles – empowering *and* forceful – depending on the situation. They're the ones who have learned versatility. They've expanded their toolboxes by adding skills that complement their natural ones.

In the exercise that follows, you'll be introduced to two leaders with different styles. Think about which one is most like you as you work through it.

Leadership Styles in Action: Mary and Bob

Mary's Profile

Mary is an accomplished project manager in a large financial services firm. She has managed projects of increasing size and complexity over the past five years and has delivered top quality products on time and within budget each time. She prides herself on her ability to drive results and achieve goals that often seem impossible to others. She pays attention to detail and lets nothing slip through the cracks.

Mary was recently promoted to lead an existing business unit comprised of three directors, each of whom has three or four staff members reporting to them. She has been on the job six months and has experienced tremendous turnover and increasingly poor team morale. "I know people have a tough time working for me. I have high standards and take my job very seriously. It is frustrating for me when others don't step up to do their jobs. If people aren't doing their jobs right, I have no problem telling them how to do it – that's my job as their boss, right?" The employee satisfaction survey was administered last month and Mary is anxious about her results.

Bob's Profile

Bob is a senior director at a mid-sized health insurance company. He leads the western region client service team, providing telephone and web-based service to policy holders. He has three service managers who report directly to him plus a small team of business analysts and process consultants. Bob is well known and well liked within the organization and spends a great deal of energy being tactful and considerate of his employees, peers, and superiors.

Because of Bob's strong desire to be liked by others, decision making is difficult for him. He often delays acting on important tasks until the last minute, creating uncertainty and anxiety for his team members and peers. His need for approval and acceptance gets in the way of his and his department's success. He is interested in being promoted to the next level but has just received feedback from his boss that he is not ready for the next step. Bob is frustrated and angry and is considering leaving the firm.

1. Which leadership style is Mary displaying? Which style is Bob displaying?

2. How have these styles served Mary and Bob in the past? How does the future look?

3. What can Mary and Bob learn from one another?

FORCEFUL AND EMPOWERING LEADERSHIP STYLES

Forceful Style	Empowering Style
Leads personally	Empowers employees to lead
Clearly declares own stand	Receptive to other people's stands
Makes tough calls	Compassionate and responsive
Judgmental	Appreciative
Competitive	Team player
Intense, expects a can-do attitude	Realistic about limits
Confident	Modest
Persistent	Flexible
Forcing function	Fostering function

ACKNOWLEDGING YOUR BELIEF SYSTEM

Why do you think people are biased against the leadership style that complements their own natural one? Let's return to Ellis' ABC model. Buried somewhere deep inside your personal beliefs lie some biases about how good leaders should act. These beliefs are frequently based in early childhood experiences you had with a given authority figure, one who demonstrated an *immature* version of either the empowering or forceful style. As a reaction against the unpleasant effects of that behavior, you try to avoid inflicting that same discomfort on the people you currently lead.

For example, you might have had a particularly forceful piano teacher in your early years who made it difficult to learn, unpleasant to come to lessons, and downright frustrating for you as a young student. Your memories of the immature forcefulness of that teacher may still be causing you, as an adult, to avoid using a forceful style with your workers. Your empowering style probably has suited you well for many years, and carried you through many situations.

But looking at it objectively, you would grant that forceful leaders bring many effective qualities to their work. To avoid being forceful at *all* times simply limits your leadership scope. That suggests your biases against forcefulness are more emotional than rational. They are born out of fears based on that bad example of a forceful style, years ago.

But there are many mature ways to use forceful or empowering styles. Forceful behavior can be a great motivator of people when high performance is crucial or a deadline is imminent. Conversely, an empowering approach can help employees gain confidence or take more ownership of an idea or process.

THREE LEADERSHIP ORIENTATIONS

Forceful

Setting Expectations and Results Orientation

- What must your organization accomplish in this fiscal year?

- What specific goals will we use to measure team and individual success?

- How can you demonstrate and demand high expectations forcefully yet respectfully?

Versatile

Demonstrating Style Versatility

- Are you inner-directed or outer-directed?

- Do you choose a leadership style, or act from fear or habit?

- Are you decisive and willing to take measured risks to achieve results?

- Are you open to new approaches?

Empowering

Supporting and Holding Accountable

- What are you doing to support your own and your employees' development?

- How effective are your coaching skills: listening, facilitating, asking for input, teaching, and offering praise and recognition?

- Do you challenge your people to accomplish more than they think is possible?

Recall that a truly mature leader makes a conscious choice to use an appropriate style of leadership in a given situation. The examples above demonstrate some of the questions you might consider within each leadership orientation: Forceful, Versatile, and Empowering.

The point is clear: leaders cannot become truly mature unless they can pivot in either direction – toward empowering leadership or toward forceful leadership – as a situation warrants. But if they have not sufficiently examined the baggage inherent in their own collection of beliefs and experiences, then they will be trapped by biases, and cannot become adequately versatile.

PRACTICING VERSATILITY

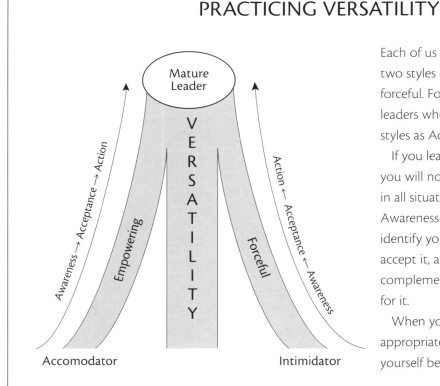

Each of us tends to naturally favor one of two styles of leadership – empowering or forceful. For teaching purposes, we identify leaders who fall into the extremes of these styles as Accomodators and Intimidators.

If you lead using only your natural style, you will not be as effective as you can be in all situations. Thus it pays to use the Awareness-Acceptance-Action process to identify your natural style, understand and accept it, and then learn to use the complementary style when situations call for it.

When you can consciously choose an appropriate style of leadership, you'll find yourself becoming a truly mature leader.

LEARNING AND PRACTICING VERSATILITY

Versatility doesn't require you to change your dominant tendency in leading. In fact, your ability to learn complementary skills will help give your natural skills greater impact.

Naturally empowering leaders who can be forceful when necessary may find that their empowering style works more effectively, because they become more decisive and action-oriented. Naturally forceful leaders who can learn to be more empowering may find that their forceful style works more effectively because they use it less often. And practically speaking, a versatile leader will find more roles to play.

Ultimately, the greatest barrier to versatility is self-doubt. If you are overly attached to either forceful or empowering characteristics, those beliefs will get in the way of your success. Overcoming self-doubt and eliminating your bias against complementary styles will help you develop a more grown-up leadership style.

You will need courage to try out and perfect new skills, especially ones that feel very unfamiliar. But with practice, you can learn to back off in some situations, to be more prying or forceful in others, and most important, to recognize the signs that something different from your natural style is called for.

The exercises that follow will help you assess your own versatility as a leader and apply Forceful, Empowering, and Versatile leadership styles in a variety of situations.

Forceful Leadership

Answer the questions below, using any format that is comfortable, e.g., bullet-points, statements, paragraphs, individual words, etc.

1. How strong are your ability and intensity regarding establishing expectations and driving results (i.e., your "achievement" thinking)?

2. Who is your best performer? List his or her top five goals for this fiscal year. How do his or her goals relate to the team's results?

3. Who is your weakest performer? List his or her top five goals for this fiscal year. How do his or her goals relate to the team's results?

4. What feedback do you need to give to your top performer to sustain his or her engagement and enthusiasm? By when?

5. What feedback and support do you need to give to your weakest performer to jumpstart his or her engagement and enthusiasm? By when?

Empowering Leadership

Answer the questions below, using any format that is comfortable, e.g., bullet-points, statements, paragraphs, individual words, etc.

1. Is coaching and developing employees a natural strength of yours? What do you base your answer on?

2. What are you consciously doing to support the continued development of your strongest employee? What new assignments could you give him or her to build his or her strengths?

3. What are you consciously doing to support the development of your weakest employee? What specific standards is he or she not achieving? What do you need to do to support, encourage, and if necessary, hold him or her accountable for achieving the standards you have set forth?

Expanding Your Leadership Versatility

Becoming a grown-up leader takes a regular, sustained approach to gaining personal insight and trying new behaviors. The following exercise assesses your own leadership versatility.

Step One

Answer the following questions and set some specific goals that will help you become a more versatile leader.

- What is your preferred leadership style: forceful or empowering?

- What is the connection between that style and your tendencies towards intimidating or accommodating behaviors?

- How do you feel about the style that complements your preferred one?

- How versatile are you today (low, medium, high)?

- What do you base your answer on?

- What level of versatility does your job require?

- What level would you like to have?

Step Two

Now, think of an example of a current work situation where you might practice more of your complementary style. Answer the following questions based on that situation:

- How could you act differently in this situation, using the complement to your natural style?

- What specific actions can you take to become more comfortable with the style you will need?

- When can you complete these actions?

- Given these steps, how do you plan to approach this situation, and what will your objectives be for the outcome?

- How will you know you made progress?

SECTION 3
RELATIONSHIP-BASED LEADERSHIP:
COACHING

"You can employ men and women to work for you,
but you must win their hearts to have them work with you."
TIORIO

ENGAGING OTHERS THROUGH RELATIONSHIP-BASED LEADERSHIP

In this section we will discuss a concept we call relationship-based leadership, which we define as leading others in a way that links an employee's purpose, talents, values and interests to organizational objectives. Relationship-based leadership, which some call employee engagement or talent management, is more than a nice way to keep people satisfied in their jobs. It's a company's ethical and business imperative that enhances productivity and affects the bottom line.

A true leader accomplishes results through others. The more senior a leader becomes, the more his or her success will be based on the ability to coach, teach, and collaborate with others. A key transition in the life of every leader is moving from a task orientation to a relationship orientation. Failure to do so will ultimately result in failure to lead. Thus, the ability to establish, leverage, and sustain relationships is a critical skill for leaders. And it's the relationship between the leader and the employee that fosters the linkage between company objectives and employee development.

We have always fundamentally believed in this link between employee engagement and organizational success. We emphasize to the leaders we work with that, by growing beyond competency with tasks, they build strong relationships with those around them to achieve big picture objectives. This relationship style, when balanced with maturity, determination and versatility, will help you successfully engage and motivate employees at all levels.

What does an engaged employee look like? Take a moment to complete the excercise on the following page, then compare your thoughts to our findings.

EMPLOYEE ENGAGEMENT AND PRODUCTIVITY

Leaders we work with say that engaged employees:

- Are clear about the purpose of their work
- Seek better ways to do their job
- Work with a high level of energy, a high need for achievement
- Are upbeat and proud to work for the organization
- Feel committed to positive team results
- Bring their full selves (i.e., brains and passions) to work regularly

A Portrait of an Engaged Employee

Reflect on individuals you are currently leading or whom you have led in the past. Pick one or two who embody your concept of an engaged employee and answer the following questions:

1. How do they go about doing their work?

2. What is important to them?

3. What motivates them?

4. How do they feel about the organization they work for?

5. How do/did they relate to you and others in their work environment?

Do you want a company full of engaged employees? Evidence suggests you should, if you want to achieve your business objectives. The link between engagement and productivity has grown well beyond a hypothesis. In recent years, solid evidence has emerged that helps define the link between employee development and business outcomes.

THE LIST OF TWELVE

Research conducted by the Gallup Organization created the following list of questions as a way to measure the elements necessary to "attract, focus and keep the most talented employees."

1. Do I know what is expected of me at work?

2. Do I have the materials and equipment I need to do my work effectively?

3. At work, do I have the opportunity to do what I do best every day?

4. In the last seven days, have I received recognition or praise for doing good work?

5. Does my supervisor, or someone at work, seem to care about me as a person?

6. Is there someone at work who encourages my development?

7. At work, do my opinions seem to count?

8. Does the mission/purpose of my company make me feel my job is important?

9. Are my co-workers committed to doing quality work?

10. Do I have a best friend at work?

11. In the last six months, has someone at work talked to me about my progress?

12. This last year, have I had opportunities at work to learn and grow?

We find the Gallup study, examined in depth in *First, Break all the Rules (FBAR)* by Marcus Buckingham and Curt Coffman, particularly useful because it moves far beyond many of the generalizations present in business today. Rather than simply concluding that engaged employees are more likely to remain in a job longer, their findings concluded that "turnover is mostly a management issue. If you have a turnover problem, look first to your manager." To us, that sounds like a problem that requires relationship-based leadership as a solution.

a direct impact on employee *behavior*, which in turn had bottom-line impacts for companies.

So now we have evidence. Companies find that they have more productive employees, less turnover, and a more positive work environment if they strive for employee engagement through relationship-based leadership. Unfortunately, the leadership model we often see is not relational at all. One-on-one meetings and interactions between leaders and employees focus more on how well the employee is accomplishing tasks and on progress reports on projects, with little or no focus on the relationship between the leader and employee. Often, these meetings are cancelled or repeatedly rescheduled, putting further stress on the relationship.

Growing up as a leader includes learning to be collaborative, relational, and versatile. It's clear that today's fast-changing business environment demands that leaders become as expert at people management as they are about their products and services. If we recognize the importance of engaging employees in achieving bottom-line results, then we must also recognize that engaging them is the responsibility of those who lead.

DEVELOPING A RELATIONSHIP-BASED APPROACH

Mature leaders recognize that the process of engaging people in their work requires ongoing efforts to build authentic relationships. But this requires more than lip service.

Our own research indicates that certain behaviors help leaders engage employees and improve their productivity. Practicing these behaviors will help you create an environment in which employees feel engaged. Do you want to grow as a relationship-based leader? Here are some suggestions you can use to cultivate stronger connections with people you lead:

- Demonstrate that employees' work makes a difference, and that they are noticed.
- Notice how employees are developing in their work, and actively encourage further growth.
- Make an effort to get to know team members as individuals.
- Share insights that help employees understand their own talents and capabilities.
- Define expectations in a way that increases clarity of tasks and responsibilities.
- Demonstrate that you seek out and take employees' opinions seriously.

Too often, leaders view interacting with employees as a bother or interruption. Such thinking is fundamentally wrong. To be a grown-up leader, you must recognize that a passion for working with and developing your employees is at the very heart of your success. Remember, you achieve results through others. Therefore, your job must include tasks such as:

- Aligning your staff around a common direction
- Working with your people to set challenging, meaningful goals
- Providing frequent and meaningful feedback
- Understanding your employees' talents and aspirations
- Helping to link those talents to company objectives

If you do not want to do these things, you do not want to lead. However, if you *do* want to be a grown-up leader, you need to focus on actions that will positively affect the attitudes of employees. Research indicates that you will be rewarded with greater loyalty, productivity and achievement of objectives.

GETTING THINGS DONE THROUGH OTHERS

As we've noted earlier, leaders accomplish results through other people. Beyond simply putting the right people on their teams, mature leaders need to get the most out of their employees, encouraging them to be as productive as possible. Enhancing productivity often means recognizing untapped potential. As a leader, your challenge is to share your experience and expertise with employees in ways that engage them and help them grow into the next generation of leaders. Ways to do this include:

* Encouraging employees to become involved in projects that stretch their skills, providing coaching and guidance so they succeed
* Showing an interest in details about employees' lives, remembering key information and following up
* Giving appropriate praise or credit when deserved, in front of others when possible
* Providing an unexpected reward to recognize hard work completed, or exceptional stress
* Inviting staff to participate in meetings, teams or task forces that might expand their horizons

ENGAGING THROUGH COACHING

By effective coaching, you can retain, engage, and grow your best employees. You can also deal with poor performance issues by identifying underlying causes of problems and devising effective solutions. Most important, you can help your team members prepare for the tasks that need to be accomplished when you are on the sidelines.

Many leaders fail to effectively engage their employees because they don't make coaching a high enough priority. We often see leaders in our coaching practice who get caught in activity traps, dealing with daily activities themselves, handling their own deadline-based work, or focusing on a stack of urgent projects that all demand immediate attention.

Leaders whose daily work keeps them from executing through others are the ones who tend to remain stuck. They haven't yet made the radical shift from a focus on tasks to a focus on relationships. They have yet to understand that they can accomplish their objectives better through other people.

The exercise that follows provides conversation starters to help you begin engaging your employees.

Engaging an Employee

Step One

Schedule a coffee or lunch appointment with a valued employee on the subject of employee engagement. In this process, we encourage you to share some of your own experiences (neither advice nor expectations) as well. Below is a list of questions that will help you start a dialogue.

- What are the three to five most important talents you bring to your job?

- What talents are most important for success in your job?

- What projects or tasks are the most satisfying for you at work?

- What engages you most at work?

- What accomplishments in the last year are you most proud of?

- What are you interested in learning more about?

- At work, things are easiest when:

- At work, things are hardest when:

Step Two

After the meeting, take a few minutes on your own to process the information you learned. What are some specific steps that you can take to help your employee become more productive or effective at work?

So, are you stuck in a whirlwind of daily activities that keep you from successfully engaging your work team? Here are some questions to ask yourself if you need help in adjusting from an activity track to a leadership track:

- How can I make my people more knowledgeable and confident, and thus more productive?
- How can I provide my employees with opportunities to learn, grow, and feel more powerful in achieving our organization's success?
- How can I delegate work to free up my time for more important tasks?
- How can I shift my employees' expectations that I must always be involved when they could take responsibility and act on their own?

Coaching is one of the best investments leaders can make with their valuable time, because it focuses on helping their employees maximize professional performance.

Everyone can learn to become a better coach. In this section we will share examples, suggest guidelines, and help you set up engaging coaching sessions with your employees. We emphasize coaching approaches that encourage honesty, congruence, mutual respect, and understanding. Whether you are an Accommodator or Intimidator, whether your leadership style tends to be forceful or empowering, our suggestions will help you improve your coaching skills.

CREATING THE RIGHT MINDSET

Now that you've committed to setting up a coaching structure with your employees, it's time to focus on creating the conditions that will make your coaching sessions meaningful and worthwhile.

We work with our clients to develop a particular mindset concerning coaching. It's an approach that encourages employees to participate fully. We also teach specific learning and questioning skills that can be particularly valuable in coaching situations. The combination is extremely fruitful.

You will notice that the coaching process creates trust and good will. To be sure you are in top form, check the following Four Mindsets for Positive Coaching Environments and assess your performance. What changes do you want to make?

As you meet with your employees, emphasize curiosity over judgment. This is a difficult area to work on, and you can expect to feel uncomfortable at first. It will help you to remember that your goal is progress, not perfection. Your new capacities for accepting yourself will come in handy here, and feedback from employees should give you additional direction.

FOUR MINDSETS FOR POSITIVE COACHING ENVIRONMENTS

Mindset #1: Show Unconditional Respect and Positive Regard

- I start out with the assumption that I hold each employee in high esteem as a person.

- I may disagree with an employee's performance, opinions or values, yet respect them as a person.

- I start challenging comments with "With all due respect..."

Mindset #2: Listen with Empath

- The employee talks. I listen.

- I ask open-ended questions.

- I "step into" the employee's shoes. I am curious but not judgmental.

- I paraphrase the employee's statements, expressing both feeling and content.

Mindset #3: Act with Integrity

- I express my thoughts and feelings respectfully and directly.

- I walk the walk, not just talk the talk.

- I speak about my values.

- I act true to my values.

Mindset #4: Lead for Development

- I leverage the talents of each employee.

- I identify employee development desires and needs.

- I demonstrate versatile leadership (both forceful and empowering).

SKILLFUL QUESTIONING

When you use questions to learn about the ideas and opinions of others, you encourage openness and engagement from your people. Questions have the ability to focus attention and increase our awareness. Use the power of asking instead of telling. A good question:

- Provides opportunity for learning both ways
- Conveys respect and confidence in others
- Creates openings for new ideas
- Allows for exploration

Open questions tend to give the other person room to roam. They require descriptive answers, promote awareness, and are much more effective in the coaching process for generating responsibility. Closed-ended or "yes/no" questions, while effective during cross-examinations, are too absolute for accuracy, and close the door on exploration of further dialogue. We suggest avoiding questions that begin with the word "why," simply because they tend to encourage defensive reactions.

SKILLFUL LISTENING

Good listening skills are fundamental to leading and coaching. One reason listening is so difficult is that you can set the right conditions, use the right words and still have trouble communicating well with your employees, especially if you don't show you are listening. Body language plays a huge role, demonstrating that you are physically and emotionally present as a listener. Use encouraging statements such as: "This is interesting." "Tell me more." "That's right."

   You may pride yourself on your listening skills. To be sure you are in top form, check the following "Don't" list below and rank your performance. If you spot any shortcomings, try the remedies on the "Do" side. Practice behaviors that demonstrate active listening as well.

DON'TS AND DO'S FOR LISTENING

Don't!	**Do!**
• Look bored, disinterested, or judgmental; avoid eye contact; turn your body away	• Make good eye contact, avoid distracting behavior, try to make your face expressive
• Shift focus to yourself and talk about your own accomplishments	• Keep the focus of all comments on other person
• Fail to acknowledge the other person's ideas or feelings, make quick judgments, give unsolicited advice, lecture	• Acknowledge and try to imagine the other person's ideas and feelings, probe for information before making recommendations
• Fail to see the other person's point of view or understand their feelings	• Ask open-ended questions to learn more and avoid jumping to conclusions
• Fail to ask follow-up questions to learn additional information, or ask only yes/no questions	• Restate what you think the other person said and keep broadening your understanding
• Fail to check whether the message was received accurately	• Ask for ideas from the other person before providing alternatives
• Narrow the choices by suggesting solutions too early in the discussion	• Allow the other person to pause, reflect, and formulate ideas before speaking
• Check your watch, answer your phone, scan emails while you are "listening"	• Clear you mind of your internal chatter and really focus on what the other person is saying

---

HOW TO SHOW YOU ARE ACTIVELY LISTENING

What do you want to show?		How do you show it?
Alertness	→	Make eye contact
Receptivity	→	Sit straight or lean forward
Interest	→	Nod
Concern	→	Use hand gestures
Involvement	→	Ask questions
Openness	→	Take notes

PRACTICALITIES OF COACHING

Nearly all our clients want to know the most practical information about coaching sessions. Here are some specific coaching do's and don'ts.

- **Do** keep a session to 15 to 45 minutes, not longer.
- **Do** hold a coaching session in your office, but not seated behind your desk. You'll want to use the position power that comes from meeting in your office, but meet at a round table or at the edge of your desk to facilitate easy discussion. The second-best option is a neutral conference room, or any room with a door for privacy.
- **Do** consider coaching to be your highest priority work and treat it with as much respect as you would a key client contact. Start and end meetings on time. Create an agenda and expect both parties to come prepared. Schedule meetings on a regular day and time so you both get in the habit of keeping the time sacred.
- **Don't** answer your telephone during a meeting. And don't postpone or cancel a meeting with an employee unless it's an absolute emergency.

The following exercise will help you prepare for and conduct a coaching meeting with an employee. It will also help you asssess how the conversation went and plan for next steps.

Preparing for a Coaching Meeting

Holding regular coaching meetings will help you get better at coaching. The following exercise will help you by suggesting a process that you can use to prepare for and learn from these meetings.

Before the meeting:

- Schedule an individual meeting.
- Set some goals for that meeting. How will you approach them? Make notes about questions that you want to ask. Pay attention to open-ended phrasing.
- Prepare for the meeting in advance, gathering any necessary data, such as feedback from other parties. You may ask your employee to prepare as well, perhaps by writing or thinking about answers to some questions that you pose.

During the meeting:

- Focus on the four mindsets of effective coaching (see page 49).
- Practice the listening and questioning skills in this section and stay focused on your employee.

After the meeting:

- What did you notice about your behavior?

- How pleased were you with the process and outcomes?

- What did you think went well?

- What might you try to do differently in future meetings with that employee, or with other employees?

- What felt comfortable about this process?

- What felt uncomfortable about this process?

- How do you think the employee felt about the meeting? (Consider following up with him or her if you're not sure about the answer.)

- What next steps will you take to continue your coaching work with this person?

COMMON CONCERNS ABOUT COACHING

This bears repeating: Every leader needs to set aside time for coaching. So when we hear some of these concerns, here's how we respond:

I don't have time for coaching.

Coaching is part of your job. If you can't make time for it, then you don't really want to be a leader, you want to be an individual contributor. All great leaders consider the development of people to be one of their top priorities because they recognize the role that those people play in realizing objectives.

I'm not qualified to coach my people.

Coaching is a learned skill. Perfection is not required before you start. As the Nike folks say, "Just Do It." You'll get better as you go. There are books, classes and seminars to help you learn, if you need to. We believe you'll improve dramatically simply by practicing the skills in this section.

I'm not a therapist. I don't do "touchy-feely."

We're not talking about therapy, but we *are* talking about connecting with your employees, which is an important part of your job as a leader. Discomfort is not an excuse to keep you from doing what you need to do. If you're uncomfortable with it, figure out why, and then take steps so you become more comfortable.

I'm not a good coach for certain kinds of employees.

All the skills that you have learned and developed to this point, as well as all your leadership experience, will help you coach your people. Your newfound awareness and acceptance of your own tendencies and biases will help you understand and relate to those same tendencies and biases in each of your employees. The insight you've gained into your accommodating style, for example, will be a great tool when coaching an assistant manager who is also an Accommodator. Conversely, if the manager is an Intimidator, you can coach for versatility by citing contrasting examples from your own natural style.

SECTION 4
RELATIONSHIP-BASED LEADERSHIP:
TEAM EFFECTIVENESS

*"Teamwork is the quintessential contradiction of
a society grounded in individual achievement."*
Marvin R. Weisbord

BUILDING AND LEADING EFFECTIVE TEAMS

Earlier, we discussed the notion of being invited to sit at the grown-up table at family gatherings. Let's take this analogy one step farther. Let's suppose that you have been appointed as the leader of the group seated at the grown-up table. In our practice, we think of teams within an organization as groups of adults sitting around grown-up tables. Some teams are highly functional, vibrant, exciting, and capable; while others are childish, petty, and downright frustrating, not to mention ineffective. Leading these teams calls on all of the abilities, skills, and knowledge that we've discussed in this workbook thus far.

The purpose of this section is to help you understand the dynamics of team leadership. In it we will offer you core knowledge, wisdom, experience, and expertise regarding how you can build and lead functional and productive teams in your organization. Almost every topic we've previously discussed in this workbook will contribute to your ability to successfully lead a team.

WHAT IS A TEAM?

Before we proceed, let's clarify what we mean by a "team." In most organizational settings, a team is a group of people who must work together in order to accomplish a specific purpose, one which they all presumably care about and agree upon.

Some groups or teams exist mostly because everyone reports to the same manager. The team members' roles do not overlap much, and team meetings are mostly opportunities for information sharing. If you are leading this type of team, your job is easier – your primary job is to make certain that you run good meetings, facilitate sharing of data and ideas, and seize opportunities to manage the group efficiently.

Organizations and leaders also form teams to accomplish objectives that none of the members could accomplish on their own. Consider a team formed to create a new manufacturing process. As the team leader, your objective won't be realized unless you can build a productive group. So your job goes well beyond thinking about manufacturing – you are challenged to:

- Help team members build productive relationships with each other.
- Draw out and resolve differences about how to accomplish the task.
- Create an environment where team members are motivated and excited about their work and take responsibility for contributing their best efforts.
- Encourage innovation.
- Guide the team through the larger organization that you serve.

ENVIRONMENTAL INFLUENCES THAT AFFECT TEAMS

No team operates in a vacuum. We recognize that there are many outside influences that can affect how a team carries out its work. In a perfect world, we should empower teams to operate as their own independent entities as much as possible. But this is not the typical situation. External influences often become barriers to a team's success.

Team leaders need to assume the task of examining systems outside of the team that may impact their work. Failure to do so can substantially limit your effectiveness. Consider these examples of how outside influences affect teams:

- **Too much attention.** A product development team in the medical devices industry has been working on an important and innovative product to bring to market. The initial results have become so impressive that the CEO has taken an even greater interest in the team's work, and now considers the device his "pet project." Both the leader and members are feeling a greater amount of pressure, and are concerned that the CEO will become the real decision-maker in their group.
- **Too little attention.** Team A shares key members with Team B, which is led by a more senior company leader. The shared members are clearly investing more time and energy in their work with Team B. As a result, Team A's meetings are poorly attended, resulting in poor progress towards its goals.
- **Unhealthy competition.** A sales team at a printing company has become so successful that some of its members have begun to look down on their colleagues on other sales teams. This elitism has become a problem within the company, fueling resentments and potentially affecting the quality of the company's work. Yet the owner needs the "numbers" that this team has been able to generate, and is hesitant to take any action that would affect their productivity.
- **Inadequate resources.** A team really needs an engineer who can fill a key role, but the engineering department is running lean, and the individual assigned isn't able to fully participate in the team's work.

Team leaders need to recognize and address outside factors that will impact their ability to function. This means ensuring that team members are able to commit to the team, that the appropriate skills are represented, that adequate resources are available to accomplish its goal, and that the appropriate levels of organizational authority are present within the team.

The next several pages describe the six critical success factors of Team Effectiveness in more detail. The exercises give you an opportunity to consider each success factor in the context of your own team.

TEAM EFFECTIVENESS MODEL

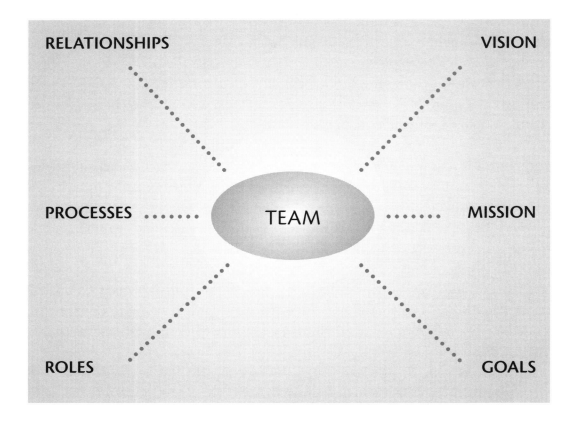

Team effectiveness involves both the leader and members in a process of creating, and then continually refining, these six critical success factors.

- **Vision** articulates success
- **Mission** describes the reason for a team's existence
- **Goals** provide a mechanism for measuring progress
- **Roles** describe the contribution of each team member toward achieving the team's goals
- **Processes** govern how the team will function
- **Relationships**, based on mutual respect, are key to effective team function

1. VISION: DEFINING SUCCESS

Vision articulates success. A team's vision should describe, as specifically as possible, what team success looks like. The purpose of vision is to motivate team members towards greater effort and achievement, and to align team members towards a common definition of success. Vision is like the North Star, offering both direction and inspiration.

A team actually needs two visions for success. The first describes successful results. For example, a team creating a new brand identity might define successful results as gaining a clear understanding of how the company is perceived by its key stakeholders and developing a focused plan to reach high potential prospects.

The second vision describes how the team wants to work together. Each team member will bring to the team his or her previous experiences with working on teams.

Early in the team's life, spend time asking each team member to describe his or her best team experience. As each team member describes his or her "personal best," listen for similar themes that all can agree on for how the team you are creating should work together. That way you can be certain that all team members are committed to creating a shared team experience, rather than having each team member trying to re-create his or her own personal definition of effective team work.

Vision Exercise

Fast forward five years and imagine you are reading an article published about the recent success of your team.

- What are the headlines and highlights?

- What challenges did you overcome?

- What attributes of your team contributed to your success?

2. MISSION: TEAM PURPOSE

Mission describes specifically the reason for the team's existence. In order to define its mission, or purpose, you need to help the team answer the following questions:

* **What?** What specifically does the team produce?
* **Who?** For whom does the team produce its products, services or outcomes? Who are your team's key customers and stakeholders?
* **How?** What unique production methods or processes are employed in creating the team's output?
* **Why?** What personal reasons do team members have for feeling passionate about producing the team's output?

In an effective team,

* The mission is understood by all members.
* It is aligned with the mission of the larger organization.

It's vital to facilitate group dialogue that will help team members shape and understand the team's mission. Involve everyone in the discussion, because misunderstandings about the mission or disagreements about the scope of the team's work can inhibit its progress.

Mission Exercise

Select two or three leaders in your organization and talk with them about the missions of their teams.

* Can they clearly articulate them?

* How would you describe the success of their teams?

* How is having a clearly defined team mission related to team success?

3. GOALS: WHAT PROGRESS LOOKS LIKE

Vision and mission are important for pointing a group in a single, agreed direction. Goals provide a mechanism for measuring whether the group is making progress in that direction. Think about taking a road trip with your friends or family. Assume your destination (or vision) is San Francisco, California. If you start out from New York City, you might set a goal of reaching Indianapolis for your first night. Now, imagine if this first night's goal had not been discussed in advance, and the driver instead takes the road to Nashville. Group frustration often results from a lack of team unity regarding the road map. The ability of a group to formulate goals and agree on means and measures of progress toward them is critical for a team's success.

In an effective team,

* Members are involved in setting goals.
* Goals are understood by, and agreed upon, by all members.
* Goals are set and met within realistic time frames.

Encourage lively discussions and even debates to reach agreements about team goals. Work to ensure that goals are realistic, and encourage members to fully commit to understanding and achieving those goals. Build and maintain team morale by measuring progress towards team goals, and plan for celebrations when you achieve certain landmarks.

Goals Exercise

Consider one outcome that you and your team must achieve this year and note the following:

* What is to be achieved?

* What are your measures of success?

* What resources and skills do you need to achieve the goal?

* How willing and able is the team to achieve the goal?

* What is the timeline for achieving the goal, including deadline and interim milestones?

4. ROLES: WHO DOES WHAT

Once team goals are established, each member needs to know his or her role within the team, and specifically what he or she can do to contribute to achieving the goals. Different from job descriptions, roles are the result of a negotiation between each team member and the rest of the team.

Team members often have unexpressed expectations for each other, which need to be aired, discussed, and clarified. Failing to clarify expectations can lead to frustration, mistrust, and the failure to accomplish important tasks.

In an effective team,

* Roles are well defined and don't overlap.
* Team members and leaders clearly understand and accept them.
* Team members and leaders accept the tasks and assignments that fit their roles.
* Members and leaders are accessible and help each other.

It's very important for you to clarify your own role as leader of the team, regarding such things as your role in team meetings, resolving disagreements, and making decisions. Failure to define your role can affect team development and even lead to power plays for authority. As leader, you must have clearly defined responsibilities, especially in the early stages (more on this later), and you must also help team members understand their own roles as the team evolves.

Roles Exercise

Describe the role you play with your own team. Be as specific as you can.

* What parts of your role are clear to you and your team members?

* What parts of your role needs further clarification?

* How does your role affect the roles of others on your team?

---

5. Processes: accomplishing the team's work

Processes develop as teams work together. Processes are the rules a team uses for meetings and individual member interactions. Explicitly discussing and agreeing on your team's processes, rather than simply letting them evolve into less-than-constructive behaviors, will increase the likelihood that your team will effectively accomplish its mission.

In an effective team,

- Decision making is timely, involving the appropriate team members.
- Meetings are efficient, with an emphasis on solving problems.
- Discussions proceed with all members listening and participating.
- Members stay informed via minutes and other communications.
- All members establish and keep deadlines and milestones.

You will need to help your team set up ground rules, and gain group agreement on those rules, in order to keep meetings effective and support productivity. Be clear about expectations regarding attendance, timeliness, and enforcement of ground rules. You'll also need to lead the group in deciding how decisions will be made. Make sure you abide by the rules: some team leaders are the busiest members, and are the ones most likely to show up late or miss a deadline.

Processes Exercise

Choose two or three team members and interview them about their experience participating on your team.

- What would they stop, start, or change relative to the team's functioning?

- What themes stand out in these discussions?

- What are one or two small changes you could make that would have a big impact on your team's effectiveness?

6. RELATIONSHIPS: THE QUALITY OF TEAM MEMBER INTERACTIONS

In order to function effectively, team members must respect each other and be able to speak openly with each other. This does not mean that team members must be best friends.

Most often, when team member relationships are strained, the reason has less to do with personality conflicts than with disagreements or lack of clarity about team vision, purpose, goals, roles, and processes. The lack of clarity results in frustration, and relationships can deteriorate quickly.

The solution to strained relationships and low trust is not to go bowling or have a pizza party. When relationships are strained, a more successful approach generally involves reviewing the team's vision, purpose, and goals and looking for misunderstandings, disagreements, or lack of clarity.

In an effective team,

* Relationships flourish: team identity and pride are evident.
* Members show tolerance for conflict, with emphasis on resolution.
* Members enjoy (or appreciate) and support each other.
* Conflict leads to growth or learning.

By being a leader who works to ensure a group focus on mission and vision, and by clarifying goals, process and roles, you will help your team members build good relationships. Competition and personality conflicts can get in the way of achieving team goals. You can take specific steps to keep everyone on task, such as modeling mature leadership styles and coaching individual team members to both participate and perform.

If you follow the discipline of working through these steps, we guarantee you that you'll see improved teamwork.

Relationships Exercise

In your next meeting, deliberately observe the relationships among team members.

* How would you describe the state of the union on your team?

* As you consider the six elements of an effective team, where do you need to turn your focus in order to improve the state of the union?

STAGES OF TEAM DEVELOPMENT

Most seasoned leaders find that learning about group dynamics enhances their leadership skills. Leaders who understand how teams develop over time, and what teams need from their leaders during different stages of development, are better prepared to help them succeed.

Here's a dynamic that we find most helpful, which has been supported by numerous studies. Teams typically evolve through four stages: they form, storm, norm, and perform. Teams that get stuck in one stage too long will have trouble achieving any of their goals. Each stage is accompanied by an increase in team productivity.

As we define each stage of team development, we'll share some characteristics of that stage, and also show how your maturity, versatility, and relational skills can help you navigate these stages and help your team gain confidence, effectiveness, and productivity. The information and exercises that follow will set you up for this development process.

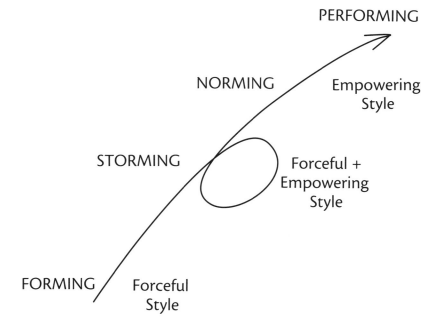

THE FOUR STAGES OF TEAM DEVELOPMENT

PERFORMING

NORMING   Empowering
                    Style

STORMING   Forceful +
                  Empowering
                    Style

FORMING / Forceful
           Style

You will find that different leadership styles will be most effective at different stages of a group's development.

Source: Bruce Tuckman

STAGE 1: FORMING – ORIENTATION TO GROUP AND TASK

This first stage of a group's development often feels somewhat uncomfortable and leader-dominated. Members can be reluctant to contribute during Forming, causing quiet meetings that feel inefficient. By the end of this stage, members have to agree on the team's vision, mission, goals, and roles and share an understanding of how the team will proceed. During Forming, the qualities of grown-up leadership apply in these ways:

MATURITY
- Show patience and understanding.
- Provide guidance and direction.
- Rely on self-confidence.

VERSATILITY
- Use a forceful style.
- Provide structure, agendas, and articulate the team's purpose.

RELATIONSHIP-BASED LEADERSHIP
- Use relational skills and encourage participation.
- Draw out Accommodators and moderate Intimidators.

STAGE 2: STORMING – CONFLICT OVER CONTROL AMONG MEMBERS AND LEADERS

Team members become more visible, testing your authority, challenging ideas, and trying to make their own impacts on the team. This is a difficult stage if you are conflict-averse; however, the healthy disagreement at this stage is very helpful and your role in working through it is pivotal. During Storming, the qualities of grown-up leadership apply in these ways:

MATURITY
- Resist temptation to shut down conflict.
- Surface unspoken conflicts to facilitate discussion around them.

VERSATILITY
- Remain forceful but recognize and seize opportunities to empower others.
- Watch for concerns about workload as team members struggle to organize themselves.

RELATIONSHIP-BASED LEADERSHIP
- Be aware of fluctuating relationships and potential for team members to become polarized.
- Facilitate open discussions, ask questions, and encourage listening among members.

STAGE 3: NORMING – TEAM FORMATION AND SOLIDARITY

As teams gel during Norming, they begin to feel pleased with their accomplishments and enjoy the company of their colleagues. The greater good takes over individual agendas. It is important to keep the team focused and on task, encouraging team members to continue to challenge and motivate each other as the team moves towards Performing, where real excellence is achieved.

During Norming, the qualities of grown-up leadership apply in these ways:

MATURITY
- Release control and let team members shine.
- Openly share issues, delegate tasks, and work behind the scenes to keep people focused.

VERSATILITY
- Sit back and reflect about the team's direction while empowering team members to move ahead.
- Use a forceful style as needed to keep team focused.

RELATIONSHIP-BASED LEADERSHIP
- Challenge the group to be open about issues and concerns.
- Offer and request constructive feedback about the team; encourage others to lead.

STAGE FOUR: PERFORMING – GROUP DIFFERENTIATION AND PRODUCTIVITY

Teams reaching this stage are highly productive and effective: members thrive within their roles, encourage others to excel, commit high levels of energy to tasks, and accomplish challenging goals. The role of the leader is to consistently challenge the team and keep them focused on team objectives. During Performing, the qualities of grown-up leadership apply in these ways:

MATURITY
- Use an empowering leadership style.
- Trust the group and recognize members' contributions, encouraging them to grow and develop.

VERSATILITY
- Look for opportunities to increase the team's scope and build links to the outside organization.
- Turn attention to new priorities as the team flourishes.

RELATIONSHIP-BASED LEADERSHIP
- Continue to coach and develop team members for future roles.
- Manage the completion/disbanding process; celebrate achievements.

Defining Team Processes

All teams have group processes. Some of those processes simply evolve after a few meetings, and aren't always helpful to the team's work. If people don't arrive on time, for example, then an expectation builds that members can show up late. Similarly, if certain members don't attend, and that issue isn't dealt with, then other members may begin to consider the meetings optional.

Effective leaders will help their teams consciously examine processes instead of letting processes evolve unchecked. Team processes include norms (or ground rules), decision-making expectations, and meeting protocols. Take some time with your team to define these processes as a group, making adjustments as necessary. Encourage your members to commit to them through future team meetings and activities.

Team norms: Team norms are basic ground rules to be followed when the team meets. Once the norms are agreed to, the team should review them at the beginning of each of its meetings, and also use them for periodic evaluation of how well the team is doing in following the norms. Your norms should number between six and eight, and might include statements such as:

* Show up to meetings or send a "proxy" in your place (assuming the team has decided about the acceptability of proxies).
* Be on time.
* Listen actively in order to improve your understanding.
* Resolve conflicts.
* Before making decisions, discuss how the decision will be made (see below).

Decision making: Team members often make the error of believing that all team decisions must be made by consensus. Reaching consensus requires that every team member has his or her say and feels heard, and that a decision has been reached that all can agree and commit to. It is time consuming, sometimes impossible, and not always the best strategy. Effective teams make most decisions through discussion, negotiation and agreement, but also recognize that there are times when a decision needs to be made by the team leader or delegated to a subset of the entire team. What is most important is that teams talk about how to make important decisions before actually deciding.

* What discussions about team processes need to take place on your team?

Team meetings: Team members should discuss at the beginning of their team's "life," and periodically review, how meetings will be run. Important considerations include:

- How often will the team meet?

- What days and times will meetings be held?

- Who will set the agenda for meetings?

- How much time in meetings will be reserved for team problem solving and how much for status updates?

- What does the team expect of members in terms of their preparation before a meeting?

- Who will facilitate the meetings?

- What happens if the agenda is not completed by the end of the time scheduled for the meeting?

- How will notes of the meeting be kept?

Leading Teams

Answer the questions below, using any format that is comfortable, e.g., bullet points, statements, paragraphs, individual words, etc.

1. What key messages do I need to continually emphasize with my team to inspire team members and increase our effectiveness?

2. What "stories" can I use that will be meaningful to my team to re-emphasize the key messages?

Enhancing Team Effectiveness

Scheduling periodic team effectiveness meetings can help many teams to establish direction or renew energy. Plan a meeting with a team that you currently work with to help set, review or refocus your efforts. Follow our suggested agenda, inviting team members to answer the questions in any format that is comfortable, e.g., bullet points, statements, paragraphs, or individual words.

As the team leader, part of your job is to keep members focused on this agenda. Ensure that everyone gets a chance to participate, and that there is consensus at the end of this process.

Team Effectiveness Meeting Agenda

As a group, answer the following questions:

* What makes our team's mission exciting, meaningful, and important?

* How does our team contribute to the overall success of our company?

* What are our top five goals to measure success this year? (Make sure your goals are **SMART**: **S**pecific, **M**easurable, **A**chievable, **R**elevant, and **T**ime-bound.)

* At what stage of development (Form, Storm, Norm, Perform) is our team operating? How do we know?

* What action(s) must we take to move to the next stage?

For additional material on team effectiveness, see pages 84-85.

SECTION 5
A MODEL FOR PERSONAL CHANGE

"You cannot act or be treated in ways that are different from those you are used to – even if those ways are better – without becoming increasingly uncomfortable."
TOM RUSK, M.D.

CREATING YOUR ACTION PLAN FOR PERSONAL CHANGE

Now that you are familiar with the fundamentals of Grown-Up Leadership – maturity, versatility, coaching, and team effectiveness – it is time to decide upon and commit to the changes you wish to make in your own leadership style and approach. This section focuses on the goal setting, action planning, and support systems that are essential to creating and sustaining change.

Change happens through curiosity and awareness. By becoming more aware of your behavior, you can choose whether or not the payoff is worth the pain of making the change. Sustainable change comes from an inner desire to make the change; changes made as a result of outside demand are more often short-lived. The Awareness-Acceptance-Action (AAA) change model introduced in Section 1 (pages 26-28) requires you to actively set new goals, seek out ways to behave differently with others, acknowledge discomfort, and invest energy in taking new risks to continue on your course of development. In return, you will emerge from this process having made real changes in your work, career, and life.

IDENTIFY DESIRED OUTCOMES

As you begin to develop your plan, consider what success will look like at the end. How will your behaviors evolve and change? How will these changes impact the people you lead and interact with? How will the quality of your relationships change? What outcomes do you want to accomplish? Think of outcomes as the broad brush strokes in the picture of how you want things to be in the future. Commit yourself fully to reaching these outcomes and keep them front and center in focus as you move forward.

SET CLEAR GOALS

Once you have identified clear outcomes, break it down even further to specify the development goals that will contribute to these outcomes. Recognize that the goals can be about enhancing a skill area where you currently have a strength as well as addressing a skill area where you have a development need. By limiting yourself to a few goals you can remain focused and progress at a measured pace. Once you've achieved these goals, you can set new goals to keep you on your path. Remember – you've had a lifetime to develop your current approach and behaviors – it will take time to evolve!

CRITERIA FOR GOOD GOALS

Good goals are **SMART**:

- **S**pecific – are described in sufficient detail
- **M**easurable – have clear quantitative or qualitative indicators of success
- **A**chievable – have adequate resources and support to be successful
- **R**elevant – relate directly to one or more stated outcomes
- **T**ime-bound – take place within a specified period of time

When you have completed your goals, share them with four or five people who are interested in supporting you in your development and ask for their feedback. This will help ensure that your goals are clearly stated and "SMART" and will also hold you accountable to someone other than yourself as you set out to accomplish them. Agree to check in with them at various points along the way to seek feedback on your progress.

DEVELOP AN EFFECTIVE ACTION PLAN

With clear goals in hand, it is time to plan what it will take to achieve them. What are the actual tasks and activities that will enable you to achieve each goal? How will you demonstrate behavior changes each day? What milestones will mark your progress? What additional resources do you need to achieve each goal? Aligning your time, activities, and resources with your goals is critical to effective action planning.

Effective action planning also includes trade-offs – what do you need to say "no" to in order to achieve your goals? Saying no does not come easy for many of us; it helps to have a bigger "yes" in mind. Account for contingencies in your plan as well. Anticipate what could go wrong and determine what needs to happen in that case.

In the exercise that follows, you will complete an action plan based on the insights you have gained throughout your work in this workbook. Depending on what goals you've set and how often you get a chance to practice your changes, you should set check-points to monitor your progress and even grade your success. The point is to weave this practice into your life rather than view it as a single event. And needless to say, once you've reached one goal, you're welcome to start work on the next!

Creating a Personal Action Plan

Refer back to your work on pages 29-30. Based on your insights, set one or two development goals. Avoid the tendency to overdo – one goal at a time is sufficient for most of us.

- The specific goal I would like to set for myself is:

- A realistic timeline for completion of this goal is:

- I will complete this goal by:

- The behavior I want to modify is:

- People who already behave as I'd like to include the following:

- I will practice this new behavior on or with these people:

- The books or courses that will help me learn more about the new behavior I am trying to achieve include:

- I will be successful when:

- The difference others will notice is:

BUILDING PERSONAL SUPPORT SYSTEMS

Building personal support systems is of great importance when embarking upon a path of change and personal development. Most people need encouragement and feedback in order to change deeply held patterns or beliefs in their lives. Also, the risk of returning to old habits is greater if you do not have a support system in place when you undertake significant changes in your life. In addition, strong support systems contribute to a happier and healthier life for most people.

We envision several aspects of support. While there may be some overlap between the different aspects, each serves a different purpose.

SPIRITUAL SUPPORT

One aspect is spiritual support – nourishing your soul, or your "being," as well as your physical body. This includes such practices as meditation, journaling, prayer, reflective reading, regular exercise, and sound nutrition. These practices help you get to know yourself and cope more effectively with life's stresses.

EMOTIONAL SUPPORT

Another aspect is emotional support – people in your life who are interested in your development, who will listen to you, and will offer "unconditional positive regard." Sources of emotional support may include close friends, a personal coach, a 12-step program, or a relationship with a skilled therapist. While significant others and family members can also offer emotional support, it is important not to rely on them exclusively.

SOCIAL SUPPORT

Social support, a third aspect, involves participating with others in activities of mutual interest and enjoyment. This could mean going out to lunch, dinner, or coffee with friends on a regular basis or having someone to play sports or games with, talk about a book with, or whatever. The point is finding enjoyment in the company of others.

PROFESSIONAL SUPPORT

The final aspect is professional support – people who will serve as sounding boards for you when you have a difficult decision to make or when you are faced with a tough problem or sticky issue to address. This is often the role of a mentor, personal coach, or a good boss. The important point is objectivity and detachment from the outcome.

Strong support systems in all these areas are critical to your sustained growth and ability to change. Reflecting on and strengthening your support systems is a worthy investment of your time and energy.

The exercise that follows will help you assess your personal support system.

Evaluating and Enhancing Your Personal Support Systems

In this exercise, you will evaluate each element of your personal support system on a scale from 1 to 5, where 1 = Unsatisfactory and 5 = Excellent. Indicate your rating by shading in the segments up to the appropiate line. When you've completed all eight segments, take a step back and look at the entire picture. If this represents the wheel of your life, how smooth or bumpy is your ride?

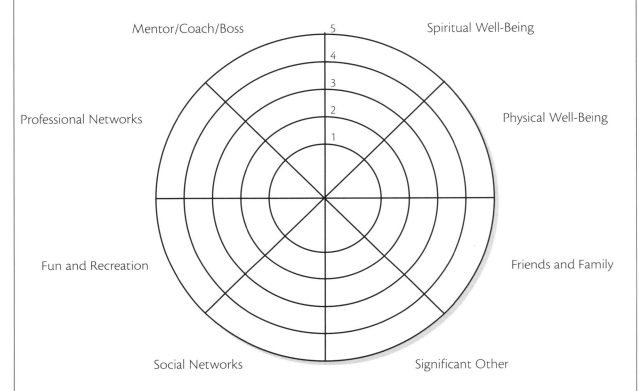

- Where do you want to make changes?

- In those areas, what are one or two practices you are willing to experiment with for the next two weeks?

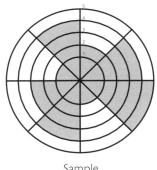

Sample

- What other actions will you take to enhance your current support systems?

SECTION 6
THE ROLE OF A LEADER

"The first responsibility of a leader is to define reality. The last is to say thank you.
In between the two, the leader must become a servant and a debtor."
MAX DEPREE

EMERGING FROM THE PROCESS

Recently, one of our clients, having successfully navigated through many of the ideas and exercises we've presented in this workbook, asked us if we believe that leaders recognize and understand the need for maturity and versatility in their jobs. Do most leaders see that a lack of self-awareness is a major barrier to their success?

Our honest response: No, there are not enough grown-up leaders out there in the world today. As long as any given roomful of people can easily come up with a long laundry list of immature leadership characteristics drawn from their personal experiences, we know that more leaders need to learn these principles. And, as we've said before, the people working for them deserve mature leaders.

Our client replied, "I'd like to go out and teach my colleagues and employees about your principles of grown-up leadership." Needless to say, that struck us as a noble and attractive idea.

But remember, while we all have big aspirations, we must remember that mastery begins at home. We certainly encourage you to share your learning experiences with others, or perhaps to discuss this workbook with them. But even if you don't do that, recall that your own grown-up leadership has a ripple effect. People notice it, respond well to it, and make changes for the better, thanks to your own growth.

DOING VS. TEACHING

In other words, you don't need to teach grown-up leadership – you need to *do* it. Because when you practice grown-up leadership, you are being authentic, and you invite authentic responses in return. When you demonstrate an ability to support, motivate *and* direct, for example, your co-workers will recognize your inner confidence, capability, and skill. When a team you lead accomplishes a major objective, or performs at a superior level for an extended period of time, those around you will notice your accomplishment. In this way your growth inspires the growth of others.

You'll see it. People will respond to your grown-up approach. They will reward you with loyalty, trust, and welcome your continued leadership. And, following their own timetables, many of them will take some of the same steps that you are taking to grow up, personally and professionally. As you lead and coach others, you will find appropriate times to encourage your employees to begin their own process of becoming grown-up leaders.

CARRYING ON

As you certainly have seen by now, grown-up leadership is a process, not an event. Even after you become aware of your own prisms and beliefs, for example, you will find that they continue to affect your actions, despite the fact that you are aware of them. After all, you've been (un)consciously maintaining them for years. Through practice, you will learn to disregard them more often when they present barriers, but they won't go away for some time, if ever.

You can expect your accommodating or intimidating tendencies to continue to pop up from time to time, too. Please don't be discouraged – this process is a normal part of growing up. Remaining grown up as a leader requires an ongoing willingness to stay connected to yourself and the people around you. As you continue down this path, challenging your beliefs and actively practicing new behaviors, you – and those around you – will encounter the Accommodator or Intimidator in their extreme forms of behavior less frequently.

We encourage grown-up leaders to continually look for ways to grow as adults. The Personal Coaching Sessions in this workbook give you exercises that you can return to regularly to reassess your situation, or to confront a particular issue you face. Keep setting personal and professional objectives, and make plans to revisit them regularly.

THE FUTURE OF LEADERSHIP

What's the ultimate benefit of grown-up leadership? By learning to be mature, versatile, and relational, you bring qualities to your workplace that are desperately needed, both today and in the future. Many of today's largest and most successful companies are allocating significant time and money trying to solve their leadership challenges. We believe that if you adopt and practice the ideas this workbook offers, your leadership will help your organization excel.

Here's why. As organizations increasingly value innovation, creativity, *and* bottom-line accountability, they count on grown-up leaders to help them balance motivation, encouragement, and expectations. They need team players who can be both forceful and empowering, who can overcome personal demons to deal with people in mature ways, and who can effectively motivate people and groups to perform at the peak of their abilities.

Grown-up leaders will be the people best equipped to meet such complex demands. We congratulate you on starting this journey!

Making an Appointment with Yourself

At least once a week, make some time to stop at a coffee shop, café, bakery or other relaxing spot on your way to work. Block out about 45 minutes and use that time to plan your day or week, write in a journal, read something uplifting or inspirational (not a newspaper or work memo), or just sit quietly while enjoying your private time.

We suggest doing this weekly for at least six weeks. The repetition will help you develop the discipline of protecting this quality time, a small personal retreat where you won't be harassed by phone calls, emails or office clutter.

Here's how our clients have benefited from this exercise.

- They become more purposeful.
- Their priorities become clearer.
- They use personal time more efficiently.
- Their perspectives on challenges seem more positive.
- They find more creative solutions, with greater ease and frequency.

Both introverts and extroverts appreciate this down time, and report feeling happier and better about themselves as a result. This is a perfect example of how spending time with yourself leads to personal growth and greater effectiveness as a leader. So enjoy the experience, and continue the process of becoming a grown-up leader.

SECTION 7
RESOURCES

GROUP SELF-ASSESSMENT FORM - OVERVIEW

The following process and form may be used throughout the life of a team to solicit feedback and generate discussion about team member satisfaction within a team meeting. Open discussion regarding how the team works together is a powerful tool for team development. Setting aside regular time to do so is important as team members may not be open to discussing their experience with the team without an objective way to offer their opinions.

Process

1. Distribute the form during the last ten minutes of every team meeting. Each team member completes the form and puts it in a pile in the center of the table. Emphasize legible writing!

2. Each team member takes one form from the pile and reads the answers from Questions 1 and 2 out loud.

3. The team leader captures ratings from Question 1 on a flip chart to calculate an approximate team average.

4. He or she repeats the process for Questions 3 and 4.

5. The leader asks the team members to read the answers to Questions 5 and 6.

6. The team leader writes the responses to Question 6 on the flip chart and brings the information to the next team meeting so the team can assess progress.

This process takes 15 minutes or less. Once the team masters the approach, it should take no longer than ten minutes to complete the assessment.

GROUP SELF-ASSESSMENT FORM

Respond to each of the following questions with your most honest answer. Please write clearly; someone else will be reading your responses.

1. On a scale from 1 to 5 with 1 being low, choose the number that best represents your level of satisfaction with your group's **processes**.

    1 · · · · · · · · · · · · 2 · · · · · · · · · · · · 3 · · · · · · · · · · · · 4 · · · · · · · · · · · · 5

2. Write a sentence or two to explain why you chose that number (the more specific you are the better):

3. On a scale from 1 to 5, with 1 being low, choose the number that best represents your level of satisfaction with you group's **product(s)**.

    1 · · · · · · · · · · · · 2 · · · · · · · · · · · · 3 · · · · · · · · · · · · 4 · · · · · · · · · · · · 5

4. Write a sentence or two to explain why you chose that number (the more specific you are the better):

5. What aspect(s) of your group's **processes** could your group profit from improving?

6. How could the group make such improvements?

This form may be reproduced for team development purposes only.

BIBLIOGRAPHY

GENERAL LEADERSHIP

Collins, Jim. *Good to Great.* Harper Business, 2001.

Gardner, Howard. *Leading Minds: An Anatomy of Leadership.* BasicBooks, 1996.

McGregor, Douglas. *The Human Side of Enterprise.* McGraw Hill, 1960.

Rucci, Anthony J., Steven P. Kirn and Richard T. Quinn. "The Employee-Customer-Profit Chain." *Harvard Business Review* (January-February, 1998, pp. 82-98).

PSYCHOLOGICAL TYPES

Briggs Myers, Isabel and Peter B. Myers. *Gifts Differing.* Consulting Psychologists Press, Inc., 1980.

Campbell, Joseph. *The Portable Jung.* Penguin Books, 1971.

Dunne, Claire. *Carl Jung: Wounded Healer of the Soul.* Continuum Books, 2000.

Hirsh, Sandra and Jean Kummerow. *LIFETypes.* Warner Books, Inc., 1989.

MATURITY

Beattie, Melody. *Codependent No More.* Harper and Row Publishers, Inc., 1987.

Chödrön, Pema. *The Wisdom of No Escape.* Shambala Publications, Inc., 1991.

Chödrön, Pema. *When Things Fall Apart.* Shambala Publications, Inc., 1997.

Ellis, Albert. *How to Make Yourself Happy and Remarkably Less Disturbable.* Impact Publishers, Inc., 1999.

Lafferty, J. Clayton. *Life Styles Inventory: LSI 1 Self-Development Guide.* Human Synergistics International, 2004.

Le Gun, Ursula. *The Wizard of Earthsea.* Bantam Books, 1975.

Maslow, Abraham H. *Toward a Psychology of Being.* John Wiley and Sons, Inc., 1968.

Miller, William A. *Your Golden Shadow.* Harper and Row Publishers, Inc. 1989.

Remen, M.D., Rachel Naomi. *My Grandfather's Blessings.* Riverhead Books, 2000.

Tharp, Twyla. *The Creative Habit: Learn It and Use It for Life.* Simon and Schuster, Inc., 2003.

RELATIONSHIP-BASED LEADERSHIP

Bridges, William. *Transitions*. Addison-Wesley Publishing Company, Inc., 1980.

Buckingham, Marcus and Curt Coffman. *First, Break All the Rules*. Simon and Schuster, 1999.

Flaherty, James. *Coaching: Evoking Excellence in Others*. Butterworth Heinemann, 1999.

Rogers, Carl R.. *On Becoming a Person*. Houghton Mifflin Company, 1961.

Rusk, Tom and Patrick D. Miller. *The Power of Ethical Persuasion*. Viking, 1993.

Salmon, Moshe. *Single Session Therapy*. Jossey-Bass Publishers, 1990.

Stone, Douglas, Bruce Patton and Sheila Heen. *Difficult Conversations*. Penguin Books, 1999.

Whitmore, John. *Coaching for Performance*. Nicholas Brealey Publishing, 2002.

TEAM DEVELOPMENT

Dyer, William. *Team Building*. Addison-Wesley Publishing Company, Inc., 1987.

Reddy, W. Brendan, Editor. *Team Building: Blueprints for Productivity and Satisfaction*. NTL Institute for Applied Behavioral Science, 1988.

Shonk, James. *Working in Teams*. Amacom, 1987.

Tuckman, B. *Developmental Sequence in Small Groups*. Psychological Bulletin (Number 63, 1965, pp. 384-399).

VERSATILITY

Goleman, Daniel. *Working with Emotional Intelligence*. Bantam Books, 1998.

Hersey, Dr. Paul. *The Situational Leader*. Center for Leadership Studies, 1997.

Kaplan, Robert E. *Forceful Leadership and Enabling Leadership: You Can Do Both*. Center for Creative Leadership, 1996.

Grown-Up Leadership

Grown-Up Leadership Workshop

The **Grown-Up Leadership Workshop** is a comprehensive leadership development program which features a proven process that enhances the effectiveness of experienced leaders at all levels. The program, customized to address the specific leadership challenges faced by leaders in the client organization, focuses on three key competencies for effective leadership: maturity, versatility in terms of leadership styles, and both coaching and teamwork effectiveness.

The design is based on The Bailey Consulting Group's proven, successful leadership coaching model and results in long-term enhanced leadership effectiveness. It features a pre-reading assignment, a 360° assessment with feedback, three group sessions, two individual coaching sessions, customized development plans for each participant based on his or her assessment results, assignments for applying the group learning back on the job, and a customized post-workshop survey which measures behavioral change and enhanced effectiveness for each participant. The workshop is constructed to allow maximum scheduling flexibility and runs over several months to allow time for behavioral changes to develop.

In addition, the data on participants can be compiled to produce a composite cultural profile which is useful in diagnosing organizational strengths and weaknesses and suggesting new leadership initiatives. The Bailey Consulting Group can also work with the senior leadership of the client organization to develop a strategy for integrating key learnings in the organization.

The **Grown-Up Leadership Workshop** helps organizations improve employee retention and engagement, breaks down "silos," enhances communication in organizations, supports change efforts, builds teamwork among managers and leaders, and can gather strategic data that helps senior leadership improve its ability to mobilize the organization for peak performance.

"The Baileys are a class act. Because they do what they advise others to do, they are authors that readers can trust. Their books are filled with ideas that challenge your thinking and that you can use immediately. I predict that the Grown-Up Leadership books will be an integral part of your leadership library."
Sandra Krebs Hirsch, best-selling author of *LIFETypes, Work It Out*, and *Soultypes*

GROWN-UP LEADERSHIP BOOKS

Grown-Up Leadership: The Benefits of Personal Development for You and Your Team

Leigh Bailey and Maureen Bailey

Why do leaders fall so short, so often? Typically, Intimidators (leaders who need to control others) and Accommodators (leaders who need acceptance) suffer equally from not knowing and accepting themselves, say leadership coaches Leigh and Maureen Bailey. Taking a holistic approach and guiding readers through a self-discovery process, the Baileys help you identify your "prism" of background and experience and see its impact on your leadership style. Then, by learning to use complementary styles and your deeper self-knowledge to coach, motivate, and direct people, you can become a truly grown-up leader. Proven, practical and positive advice, practices, tools, and stories from real people make this an inspiring, challenging book.

The Grown-Up Leadership Workbook: The Personal Growth Process for Leaders and Their Teams

Leigh Bailey

This workbook helps leaders outgrow fears and limitations as they work through a series of exercises, guided reflections, self-assessments and interactions with others on the path to their own grown-up leadership. It's a proven, holistic approach that thousands of leaders credit with making major impacts on their work and personal lives. They gain maturity, versatility and a heightened ability to coach and work productively with teams as they increase their self-awareness and escape biases and blind spots. The workbook is designed as a free-standing coaching tool that leaders can use on their own to grow up fast.

Grown-Up Leadership (ISBN 90-77256-09-1)
144 pages, (6 ½" X 9"), paperback, US$18.95
Models, charts, anecdotes, an index and other resources

Grown-Up Leadership Workbook (ISBN 90-77256-15-6)
96 pages (8 ½" x 11"), paperback, US$14.95
Information, worksheets, and resources

LEARN MORE ABOUT GROWN-UP LEADERSHIP

To learn more about **Grown-Up Leadership**, order books, or to learn about leadership coaching services offered by The Bailey Consulting Group, visit our website at www.thebaileygroup.com or contact us at info@thebaileygroup.com.

TAKING CHARGE OF YOUR CAREER

TAKING CHARGE OF YOUR CAREER WORKSHOP

The **Taking Charge of Your Career Workshop** has been successfully offered to thousands of participants by The Bailey Consulting Group in organizations during the past two decades. The **Taking Charge of Your Career Workshop** can be offered in a variety of formats including a one-day session, two half-day, or four two-hour sessions.

One of the benefits of this flexibility in format is that you can customize the workshop to meet the scheduling requirements of your organization. A second major advantage is that the workshop offers the option to add organization-specific content to the core workshop. In this way, it is possible to creat a customized version that is unique to your organization.

For example, some organizations add specific content on their internal job posting program, educational reimbursement programs, and other development policies and practices. Others have included employee panels from different parts of their organization to educate participants on various career options offered within the organization.

Another common addition to the workshop, if the organization has a qualified practitioner on staff or available as a consultant, is to offer assessments such as the Myers-Briggs Type Indicator or Strong Interest Inventory to augment the exercises in the *Taking Charge of Your Career Workbook.*

The workbook, created for the **Taking Charge of Your Career Workshop,** can be used by individuals as a self-directed learning tool, or as a participant workbook for a facilitated workshop. Many Human Resources professionals and career consultants use this workbook in their own practices as well.

By attending a **Taking Charge of Your Career Workshop**, employees will
- Gain a clearer understanding of their strengths and talents
- Assess their satisfaction with their current job and develop a specific plan to make their job more satisfying
- Learn and practice skills to establish and achieve long-term career goals
- Prepare to share with their managers the areas of growth they will work toward and the contributions they want to make

Organizations will benefit by increased employee engagement, productivity, satisfaction, and accountability as employees begin to proactively manage their careers.

TAKING CHARGE OF YOUR CAREER BOOK

Taking Charge of Your Career Workbook:
The Proven Process for Job Satisfaction

Leigh Bailey

You carry at least 70% of the responsibility for making your career satisfying and successful. So take charge! This workbook has been used by thousands to make their current jobs more satisfying and to set and achieve future job or career goals. It's based on the wisdom that you need to know your work self – your talents, skills, experience and values – in order to explore and define what work will satisfy you best. You'll find:

- Powerful, practical worksheets
- Reflection exercises
- Tips from seasoned career coaches and consultants
- Resources section
- Bibliography

It's full of the proven advice and encouragement that have already helped workshop participants reshape their work lives. Use it on your own or with your career coach to make positive changes for your future.

Taking Charge of Your Career Workbook (ISBN 90-77256-13-X)

96 pages (8 $\frac{1}{2}$" x 11"), paperback, US$14.95

Information, worksheets, and resources

LEARN MORE ABOUT TAKING CHARGE OF YOUR CAREER

To learn more about the **Taking Charge of Your Career Workshop**, or to learn about one-on-one career coaching services offered by The Bailey Consulting Group, visit our website at www.thebaileygroup.com or contact us at info@thebaileygroup.com.

GROWN-UP TALENT MANAGEMENT

Here's a telling statistic: 99 percent of corporate leaders believe they need stronger talent pools than they currently have. That's a case for expertise in talent management.

That figure, cited in *The War for Talent* (Ed Michaels, Helen Handfield-Jones, Beth Axelrod, 2001) exposes the challenge facing leadership of organizations. Though the business climate has undergone significant transition since the book was published, organizations continue to be faced with ever-increasing workloads, handled by fewer employees who work under more stress than ever before.

What companies need are teams of fully engaged employees. It's very clear that every individual's talent is crucial to meeting today's business needs. Successful organizations can't afford poor (or even mediocre) performers at any level. They need everyone, working together at full capacity, to sustain productivity. Clearly, corporate leaders feel that strain when calling for more effective workers. That's where Grown-Up Talent Management comes in.

Talent management is the process of generating full engagement and optimal use of each employee's unique talents in the workplace. Some companies rely on external stimuli such as raises, bonuses, and promotions to motivate employees, which on their own are relatively ineffective tactics for boosting performance. Numerous studies have proven that for employees to be fully effective, they need to know and accept themselves in order to find intrinsic value in their work. They must be authentically interested in and skilled in the tasks that need to get done. Moreover, they need to be supported in taking care of themselves physically, mentally, and spiritually. In this way, talents are developed into strengths and become known not only to the employee but to the entire organization. Once known, those talents propel organizations to greater productivity and profitability.

Who is responsible for talent management? Ideally, everyone within an organization should be involved, from the individual contributor to supervisors and managers to senior leaders. Individual contributors bear the greatest responsibility by far.

But to encourage employees to accept their responsibilities, managers and leaders must coach employees toward the self-discovery of their interests and talents. Great managers and leaders also clarify roles and responsibilities, helping their people recognize how they fit into the larger team. Such coaching requires much self-awareness, self-management, and relationship-based leadership!

GROWN-UP TALENT MANAGEMENT WORKSHOP

The **The Grown-Up Talent Management Workshop** offers a proven approach for teaching leaders to do their part in attracting, engaging and retaining talent in their organizations. A simple Five-Step Process for Development Coaching provides managers and leaders with a road map development planning with their employees. Through learning and practice, leaders gain new confidence and skills that make them effective talent managers, able to do their part in creating and implementing development plans which focus, empower, and retain valuable employees.

LEARN MORE ABOUT TALENT MANAGEMENT

To learn more about the **Grown-Up Talent Management Workshop**, or to learn about one-on-one career coaching services offered by The Bailey Consulting Group, visit our website at www.thebaileygroup.com or contact us at info@thebaileygroup.com.

ADDITIONAL READING
FROM NOVA VISTA PUBLISHING

www.novavistapub.com

Business books from Nova Vista take complex things and make them simple, through stories and conceptual models, so you understand WHY. They take what's hard to do and make it easy, through new behavioral and strategic tools, so you learn HOW. They make inconsistent success consistent, helping you CHANGE, grow, and feel good about work and life.

Each title underscores Nova Vista's core values: deep respect for every person, and the conviction that people work best when they feel good about their jobs and daily lives. Titles focus on leadership, sales and sales management, customer service, call centers, cross-cultural and virtual work, blended and distance learning, change, and communication styles.

Time Out for Leaders: Daily Inspiration for Maximum Leadership Impact
Donald Luce and Brian McDermott

Leaders around the world recognize that daily reflection is absolutely necessary for defining values, establishing direction and pursuing vision. Luce and McDermott, two of the world's leading international consultants in leadership development, help leaders to take ten minutes a day to focus on the principles they live by and help those around them develop and prosper.

ISBN 90-77256-10-5. Hardcover, ribbon page marker, 272 pages, US$19.95

Service Excellence @ Novell: Taking Customer Service from Cost to Profit
The Best Practices Editors of Nova Vista Publishing

Ten years ago, Novell's customer service division was pleasing customers. But in a high-impact transformation, the division raised its sights and now also contributes significantly to the company's profitability. What happened? From the executives to the front line people, everyone changed the way they work to support Novell's strategy: make customer service a differentiator to attract new customers, while growing current customers' business. A fast-reading, entertaining corporate drama told in human terms.

ISBN 90-77256-11-3. Paper, 144 pages, US$18.95

Leading Innovation: Creating Workplaces Where People Excel So Organizations Thrive

Brian McDermott and Gerry Sexton

It's critical today to find new ways to create business growth. The best answer lies in the untapped talent, creativity and passion of people. But how do you create an environment of perpetual innovation – where everyone is committed to excellence? Learn how to create a culture and mindset of perpetual innovation and ensure sustainable excellence. For leaders and managers who believe people are their organization's most important asset.

ISBN 90-77256-05-9. Paper, 160 pages, US$18.95

Win-Win Selling: The Original 4-Step Counselor Approach for Building Long-Term Relationships with Buyers (Wilson Learning Library)

A company's sales force can be a market differentiator and help it gain sustainable revenue if it adopts the Counselor approach. The Win-Win mind and skill set, based on trust, problem-solving, and side-by-side work between seller and customer, makes buying easy and opens long-term, expanding business. Gives the million-plus people in 30 countries who have taken Wilson Learning's Counselor Salesperson course a refresher, and gives new and experienced salespeople a powerful new sales process.

ISBN 90-77256-01-6; French edition 90-77256-07-5. Paper, 160 pages, US$18.95

The Social Styles Handbook: Find Your Comfort Zone and Make People Comfortable with You (Wilson Learning Library)

Backed by a database profiling more than 2 million people, Wilson Learning's Social Styles concepts are powerful, life-changing communication tools. The ways you prefer to influence others and how you feel about showing emotion identify you as an Analytical, Expressive, Driver or Amiable. You feel comfortable acting within your own style. But to relate well with others, you must consciously adjust your style to theirs. Learn your own Social Style, how to read and react to others', and how to use Versatility to handle conflict and stress.

ISBN 90-77256-04-0. Paper, 192 pages. US$19.95

I Just Love My Job: The 7P Way to Satisfaction at Work

Quarto Consulting

Presents Quarto's dynamic 7P tool for career development. Profile the drives that motivate you and learn what that means in terms of strengths and limitations. Discover what kinds of work will be fulfilling for you. Then learn how to influence people and make changes that give you more fulfillment at work. The 7Ps (purpose, positioning, plans, power, process, people and product) are a powerful conceptual framework and give new, fresh insights and encouragement for people in all phases of their careers.

ISBN 90-77256-02-4. Paper, 192 pages, US$19.95

ABOUT THE AUTHOR

Leigh H. Bailey, B.S., M.A., is the president and principal consultant of The Bailey Consulting Group. Its mission is to support individuals, teams, and organizations in realizing their maximum potential for human development and effectiveness by providing customized consulting and coaching in career, team, and leadership development and psychological type.

The Bailey Consulting Group assists clients in both large and small organizations in a range of industries including financial services, health care, mortgage banking, engineering, medical technology, and social services.

Prior to founding The Bailey Consulting Group, Mr. Bailey served as Senior Management Development Consultant at Norwest Corporation (now Wells Fargo). His primary emphasis was in leadership development, team building, career development and sales training, and he has delivered consulting, coaching and team building experiences throughout the United States. He has held positions in the financial services industry including product manager, private banker, consumer banking manager, vice president, and senior institutional trust marketing representative.

Mr. Bailey is Adjunct Program Assistant Professor of Human Development at St. Mary's University of Minnesota. He holds a M.A. degree in Human Development from St. Mary's University and a B.S. degree from the University of Wisconsin. He has done additional graduate work at the University of Minnesota and The Carlson School of Management, and has completed advanced professional training in team building and coaching. Mr. Bailey is also qualified to administer and interpret the Meyers Briggs Type Indicator (MBTI) and the Strong Interest Inventory (SII), two of the mostly widely used tools in career and team development.

The co-author of *Grown-Up Leadership* and author of *The Grown-Up Leadership Workbook* and *The Taking Charge of Your Career Workbook*, Mr. Bailey lives in Minneapolis, Minnesota, USA. His interests include wilderness canoeing, distance running, and singing.